THE
Denny's®
STORY

THE

STORY

HOW A COMPANY
IN CRISIS
RESURRECTED
ITS GOOD NAME

JIM ADAMSON
WITH ROBERT McNATT
AND ROSEMARY BRAY McNATT

John Wiley & Sons, Inc.

NEW YORK • CHICHESTER • WEINHEIM • BRISBANE • SINGAPORE • TORONTO

Published by John Wiley & Sons, Inc.

Published simultaneously in Canada.

Library of Congress Cataloging-in-Publication Data:

Adamson, Jim.
    The Denny's story : how a company in crisis resurrected its good name/ Jim Adamson with Robert McNatt and Rosemary Bray NcNatt.
      p. cm.
    Includes index.
    ISBN 0–471–36957–8 (cloth : alk. paper)
      1. Denny's, Inc.   I. Title: How a company in crisis resurrected its good name and reputation.   II. McNatt, Robert.   III. McNatt, Rosemary Bray.   IV. Title

TX945.5.D43 A33 2000
338.7616479573–dc21   99-047275

*To the 60,000 employees of Advantica
and Rachelle Hood-Phillips
who helped make this cultural change possible*

Contents

Acknowledgments

It took the efforts and commitment of our entire organization to make the tremendous business and cultural transformation at Denny's/Advantica a reality. The people listed below are those I wish to thank for their special help and encouragement. Without you, we wouldn't have been able to tell this story.

John Relman, Terry Demchak, and Brian Heffernan, who helped us begin the process.

Ron Petty, Rob Barrett, Karen Randall, Jim Gray, and the Denny's franchisees, who were there at the outset.

John Romandetti, who leads the nation's largest family restaurant chain on a daily basis.

Dory Djerf, who came with me first and continues to be a valuable asset.

Edna Morris, Karen Kanes-Floyd, Stephen Wood, Paul Wexler, Ron Hutchison, Bob Campbell, Craig Bushey, Nelson Marchioli, Rhonda Parish, Maggie Petersen-Penn,

Jim Lyons, Dora Taylor, April Kelly, Darrell Jackson, Karen Regan, and Aundrea Clark, who made significant contributions.

Henry Kravis, Paul Raether, Mike Tokarz, Cliff Roberts, George Roberts, Betsy Sanders, and Vera King Farris, who were so supportive of what we needed to do.

Ron Blaylock, Jim Gaffney, Irwin Gold, Rob Marks, Charlie Moran, Don Shepherd, and Raul Tapia, who came in later and supported all of our programs.

Rosemary and Bob McNatt, who were gifted with the ability to write and helped tell this story. Ruth Mills, who pushed us beyond our comfort zone.

Sam Chisholm and Ann Marie Gothard, who were our partners all along the way.

To 60 *Minutes*, *Fortune*, and *USA Today*, who invested the time to learn first hand our story and were willing to tell about the progress we made.

Brad Scheler, who has been my friend and advisor for a number of years.

And my family, Lyn, Ryan, and Mark, who pushed me to go forward when I had doubts that we could succeed.

Introduction

The day that Denny's restaurants became an icon for racism in the United States, I was living hundreds of miles from its South Carolina headquarters, running the Burger King Corporation in Miami, Florida. Like the rest of America, I'd heard and read news accounts about six black Secret Service officers assigned to guard the president of the United States. The men accused the servers and managers at an Annapolis, Maryland, Denny's of humiliating and discriminating against them while their white colleagues enjoyed a hearty breakfast. Even worse, the incident was the latest in what appeared to be a rash of complaints against the company.

I do remember thinking that here was a business that needed some change—and fast. But it never occurred to me, working in Miami in April of 1993, that in less than two years, Denny's problems would become mine—and that I would be privileged to help lead the work of changing

Denny's, its parent company, Advantica, and the company culture. How the company, and the team we assembled here, made this incredible change is the subject of this book.

Our challenges were many. We were the laughingstock of the nation, with everyone from Arsenio Hall to Jay Leno attacking what they saw as a stereotype of Southern bigotry and intolerance. Advantica itself was riddled with debt, the unfortunate result of a 1989 leveraged buyout that created interest payments which sucked up our profits as fast as we made them. In the early 1990s, when claims of discrimination against Denny's began to capture the public's attention, the record revealed a company culture that was locked in the past: We had virtually no suppliers who were persons of color; only one franchisee was African-American; the company's board of directors was made up primarily of white men. No one had addressed issues of race and ethnicity in training, in human resources, or in any other department. And though by the time I arrived, some steps had been taken to remedy this situation, they were simply not enough. We were a service company whose customer base was the United States itself. And yet by every important contemporary measure, we were far, far behind the curve.

But that was then, and this is now. How far have we come? Consider this:

- Of the 823 Denny's restaurants owned by franchisees, people of color own 309 of them, including Akin Olajuwon, who owns 75 restaurants, making him our second-largest franchisee overall.

- Our company does $125 million in business with minority suppliers each year. That's 18.8% of our contracts—the national average for American businesses is 3% to 4%.

- Every person employed by Denny's—from servers to security officers, from media planners to managers in our restaurants—receives specific training that emphasizes respect for differences among people and encourages our workers to value—even celebrate—those differences.

- Our current board of directors is composed of 36% people of color.

- At the senior management level, 27% of them are women and people of color.

- For two consecutive years, *Fortune* magazine has ranked us among the top 10 companies for minorities in the United States.

- After a debt-restructuring process that placed us on a solid financial footing, we are moving aggressively forward with reinvestment programs that are generating positive results. Denny's posted record systemwide sales of $2 billion and record earnings before interest, taxes, depreciation, and amortization (EBITDA) of $184 million in 1998.

What did it take to turn Advantica around? Hours and hours of hard work; the incredible skills of some dedicated men and women; thoughtful, innovative, and proactive programs; the willingness to lead and take risks; and most of all, an absolute commitment to doing what was right, no matter what.

We live in a country in which the issues of diversity and inclusiveness are now firmly on the front burner.

Companies large and small, throughout every industry, understand the importance of helping Americans of varied backgrounds respect one another and learn to work together. But as we've learned from the people who've called to ask us for advice, very few people know how to accomplish this vital goal.

We learned the language of inclusion because we were forced to learn it; and then we learned to walk our talk to survive. What we've found over these past few years is that not only have we survived, we've flourished. Inclusion and diversity are something we focus on each day; they are integral to the way we do business. Instead of being a laughingstock, we're now a model. And what we've done here can be done by any company that's committed. If you want to know how, read on.

Our Worst Hour

O n December 30, 1991, Christina Ridgeway, a student at Gunderson High School, left a symposium about college life sponsored by the National Association for the Advancement of Colored People (NAACP) and San Jose State University. The senior was looking forward to attending college and felt energized by the discussions she'd been part of at the gathering. She and a group of other high school and college students talked until the early hours of the morning, then decided to grab a bite to eat at the local Denny's restaurant.

One of the group, Eddie Lamont Jones, already in college at Tuskegee Institute in Alabama, was home for Christmas break and had attended the seminar at the San Jose Hyatt to help out. He and three of his friends were among the first of the group to arrive at the Denny's on Blossom Hill Road at about 1 A.M. When Jones approached the manager to let the staff know that their group was larger than usual, that was when Jones said their troubles began.

Even before seating the gathering group of students, Ridgeway, Jones, and others would claim, the manager began announcing the restaurant's prepayment policy and its $2 cover charge in what the students described as a loud, even hostile voice. Ridgeway, Jones, and the other teenagers said they were told stories about other groups that had left the restaurant without paying, and that when they asked to see a copy of the manager's stated policy, he refused.

Ridgeway later said that she was suspicious of the manager's claims and noticed several of her other friends—all of them white—seated in another part of the restaurant enjoying their meal. She said that when she approached that group and asked whether they had to prepay, they reacted with surprise. No one had asked them to pay in advance, they told her. Ridgeway said that while Jones and the other members of her group continued to wait, she approached the manager again and asked whether breaking up into smaller groups would solve his problem with them. She said the manager refused to budge, and in the end, they left without eating—but with painful memories. She would later describe herself in a newspaper account as humiliated and angry. "He violated my rights not only as a black person but also as a teenager."

"This Just Broke Me..."

It was late December of 1992, about 11:30 P.M., and Leon Youngblood was tired. On his way home from a business trip in San Diego, the young customer service representative for Pacific Bell decided to stop in Costa Mesa, California, for a late-night meal at Denny's on 17th Street. He stood in line at the hostess podium, waiting with a dozen other customers for a table. He watched as patron after patron was seated and noted with dismay that he was the only black person among the group. Finally, after 15 minutes of waiting, he asked employees standing nearby to seat him. But, as Youngblood later remembered, the employees only laughed at him.

Eventually, Youngblood seated himself, but he soon found that his ordeal was not over. As he tells the story, more time passed without attention from a single employee. While he watched, white patrons entered the restaurant, were immediately seated, and received both menus and food. When he confronted an employee and asked why no one would help him, Youngblood says he was told to call Denny's 800 number if he had a complaint.

In an interview with a reporter from the *San Diego Union Tribune*, Youngblood told reporter Leslie Wolf that he asked to see a manager and was told she was on break. When he requested the use of a pen to write down the toll-free number, "the employee said, 'You want to use my pen, you better say please.'" Frustrated and hurt, Youngblood left the restaurant but says the memories linger.

"I've never cried before, except at funerals, but this just broke me," he said in the newspaper article. He added that ever since his experience in a Costa Mesa Denny's, going to restaurants has made him nervous.

* * * * * *

It was a happy family group that drove to a Denny's in San Diego on the evening of November 16, 1991. The 11 adults and 2 children comprising the Maxwell family had just returned from a football game at San Diego State

University, and it was dinnertime. But when they arrived at the restaurant, they waited 30 minutes for a hostess to seat them, according to accounts from family members. Even then, the hostess seated only half their party, leaving the remainder of the Maxwell family to stand for an additional half hour. Once the rest of the group was seated, they were placed at a table far away from the rest of their family members, they said.

Once a server finally arrived to take their order, the Maxwells reported that they were asked to prepay for their meals and said they were told they could not be served until they prepaid. Demetrice Maxwell rose from her seat and approached the smaller table where other family members were seated. When she discovered that group had not been asked to prepay, she confronted the manager—who told Mrs. Maxwell that the server had indeed made a mistake: Her entire family should have been asked to prepay.

Her curiosity aroused, Mrs. Maxwell asked other customers—white customers—whether they had been asked to pay for their meals in advance. According to Mrs. Maxwell, not one of the white customers had been asked to pay first and eat later. When she pressed the manager to explain the policy, she was told that college students often came to the restaurant, ate their meals, and left without paying. Yet Mrs. Maxwell claimed that in her informal survey of college students at the Denny's restaurant, not a single white student had been asked to pay before eating.

"Her First Day as a Teenager"

December 11, 1991, was Rachel Thompson's thirteenth birthday, and all the teenager wanted for dinner was waffles and an ice cream sundae at the local Denny's. So Susan and Danny Thompson took Rachel, along with their two other children, Jason and Danny Jr., to a Denny's restaurant in Vallejo, California. The couple brought along Rachel's baptismal certificate as proof of her birthdate, to take advantage of Denny's popular promotion of a complimentary meal on the customer's birthday.

The restaurant was almost empty when the Thompsons arrived, yet it seemed to them that the server took an inordinate amount of time to approach their table. The Thompsons later said that the server who came to their table quickly spoiled their festive mood, refusing to say hello or otherwise greet them politely. Instead, she demanded to know what the group wanted to eat. The family might have ignored her behavior or chalked it up to a bad day, they said. But when they told the woman that it was Rachel's birthday and that she was entitled to a free meal, the Thompsons claimed her already unfriendly attitude became markedly colder. As they presented their daughter's baptismal certificate, family members said that she ignored the document and stormed off to get her manager's approval.

The server returned to the Thompsons' table with her manager, but the family said the situation didn't improve— in fact, it seemed to escalate. When the manager asked whether they had any proof that it was Rachel's birthday, Mrs. Thompson again presented her daughter's baptismal certificate, but the manager refused to take the certificate from her hand. She later recalled that the man told her that the baptismal certificate wasn't acceptable but that he could accept Rachel's school identification. Yet when Rachel produced the requested identification, the manager rejected it, according to the Thompson family, and asked again to inspect the baptismal certificate.

Mrs. Thompson remembered sliding the certificate across the barren restaurant table, only to have the manager rebuke her for throwing things at him. As the family watched in growing dismay, the manager began shouting at the mother. Finally, the family left the restaurant, their birthday party spoiled and, as they later said, their illusions shattered. Even years later, the Thompsons' anger and hurt were palpable.

"I was angry, outraged at what happened," Susan said in interviews. "I felt insulted. You have to have lived it to know how it felt. ... The pain [was] too great, especially on my daughter's thirteenth birthday, her first day as a teenager."

* * * * * *

On the morning of April 1, 1993, 21 Secret Service agents reported for roll call at Andrews Air Force Base in Maryland. It was 6:30 in the morning, and President Bill Clinton, the focus of their assignment that day, was set to arrive at noon in Annapolis, Maryland, 30 miles away. The president had scheduled a visit to the United States Naval Academy; the detail assembled at Andrews would be responsible for a variety of tasks necessary to ensure the safety of the president. At roll call, the advance officer notified the officers assigned to the magnetometer detail that their metal-detecting equipment, designed to screen people attending presidential functions, would need to be fully operational by 9:30 A.M. in order to handle the crush of reporters and cadets expected to attend the event. Still, the detail determined that they had an hour to get breakfast, reach the naval academy, and set up their equipment in time. It made sense for the men to stop at a Denny's restaurant on West Street, not far from the academy itself.

As the agents remember it, the room wasn't crowded at all, and the hostess directed all the officers to the same section of the restaurant, allowing them to spread out among several booths and tables nearby. Among those 21 men were 7 African-Americans; six of them—Alfonso Dyson, Melvin Fowlkes, Merrill Hodge, Joseph James, Leroy Snyder, and Robin Thompson—sat at a table together. The remaining men, including one Latino and one African-American man, sat elsewhere. The men made a striking picture as they took their places at the restaurant tables, all dressed in the Secret Service uniform common to a presidential detail: black shoes, black pants with wide gold stripes on the outside, white shirts with narrow black ties, gold badges, gun belts—and the official seal of the president of the United States.

Like all Denny's restaurants in that period, the restaurant was participating in one of the company's most popular promotions: the All-You-Can-Eat Breakfast. Customers chose five items from the menu and could eat all they wanted for a fixed price. Unlike many restaurants that offer a similar meal in a buffet setting, Denny's restaurants offered the meal cooked to order.

Many of the agents ordered the All-You-Can-Eat Breakfast. But no matter what the order, it became obvious after 30 minutes that the table with black officers was completely without food, whereas the other officers already were eating. One of the black agents, Robin Thompson, said he twice approached the server to inquire about their meals and was told to wait. After Thompson's inquiry, one of his colleagues, a white officer sitting at a booth right next to the six black agents, noticed the face of the server as she left the table. This officer, William Winans, said later that the woman rolled her eyes as she walked away from Thompson.

By this time, the black members of the magnetometer detail had been waiting 45 minutes for food, according to accounts they gave later. As they reported, they watched as patrons who entered a half an hour later than they did were served and were eating their meals even as the six men continued to wait. Not only did their nonblack colleagues report having been served promptly but several also said they had been served second helpings of their meals.

Finally, Thompson told the server that he wanted to see the restaurant manager. Meanwhile, the agents had consulted with their supervisor, James Sobers, who advised them to file a complaint against the restaurant, since there was nothing left to do given their schedule. Just as the six hungry men prepared to leave the restaurant, the server was said to have returned to their table with only one of their orders, which they were unable to eat. At about the same time, the manager approached the agents; they asked him for the name and address of Denny's regional management office. But the agents claim the manager made the mistake of giving them the address not of Denny's corporate offices but of the restaurant itself. Because the manager's native language was not English, he might have misunderstood the agents' request. Whatever the reason, the agents said they finally acquired the address of the restaurant's corporate headquarters only because of a Maryland restaurant license tucked into the window of the restaurant. Along the way, the six black men stopped for some fast food from a nearby Roy Rogers restaurant, then proceeded to the naval academy and their assignment.

"I didn't want to believe it was discrimination," Alfonso Dyson would say later. "I'm not one to cry discrimination;

it's not in my blood. But I couldn't think of what else it would be."

No Laughing Matter

Whatever else "it" turned out to be, these stories—and dozens more like them—would become a litany. They would be repeated in newspapers and magazines, on radio and television shows, across the United States and around the world. Cartoonists would sketch out their sarcastic takes on the corporate racism of Denny's restaurants. Comedians from Jay Leno to Arsenio Hall would make joke after joke in their opening monologues.

"Denny's is offering a new sandwich called the Discriminator," Leno said one night in May 1993. "It's a hamburger, and you order it, then they don't serve it to you."

Later that month, during the NBA finals, Leno joked about a news story that reported Chicago Bulls player Michael Jordan being sighted in public at 3 A.M. the night before the game. Leno said that though Jordan had planned to go home early, "he'd stopped for dinner at Denny's at about 6 P.M., but no one ever came to take his order."

The combination of hundreds of complaints, a growing number of lawsuits, and relentless publicity had turned Denny's restaurants, one of the country's largest restaurant chains, into what one person called "a poster child for racism." Like many other Americans, I was aware of the troubles at Denny's—and more than a little grateful that they weren't my troubles. From my distant vantage point as CEO of Burger King Corporation, it appeared that Denny's would have an extraordinary amount of work to do to combat the miserable image it had as a racist company. The most important thing it would have to do, I figured, would be to make sure whatever changes they planned to make were not just cosmetic ones. They'd have to change the culture of the company itself to keep allegations of racism and discrimination permanently at bay.

I couldn't really say I was sorry about not having to face such a massive job. Some of the work I imagined needed to be done, I would learn later, already was beginning at Denny's. No one could have told me that, in a few years, *I* would be the man assembling a team of people from across the country to tackle this daunting task. These men and women, along with me, would be the architects of the change that would move Denny's from being the butt of jokes to being a model for inclusion. For a long while, it would be a bumpy ride.

2

From Doughnuts to Diners

The $2 billion company I lead, now known as Advantica Restaurant Group, had its origins in a series of acquisitions that occurred throughout the 1970s and 1980s. The actual Denny's brand got its start in 1953 as a simple doughnut shop, "Danny's Donuts," in Lakewood, California. The place didn't do badly at all its first year. Its founder, Harold Butler, made about $120,000. Butler took the profits from that first year and used them to open more doughnut shops. He even expanded the menu a bit to include some sandwiches and a few entrees and renamed the enterprise "Danny's Coffee Shops." Butler never made a secret of his goals for the fledgling enterprise. He wanted, he said, "to serve the best cup of coffee, make the best doughnuts, give the best service, keep everything spotless, offer the best value and stay open 24 hours a day."

Five years later, Danny's Coffee Shops became Denny's restaurants, with 20 locations by the end of 1959. Butler, aware of the chain's potential, began a vigorous program of franchising in the early 1960s. His expansion plans focused on establishing his restaurants in strategic locations, off the budding interstate highway system—the kind of places that were a natural stop for weary travelers. By 1963, there were Denny's restaurants open in seven western states. In 1966, Denny's had grown enough to make its initial public offering on the American Stock Exchange. In 15 years, it grew to a chain of more than 1,000 restaurants, offering a complete menu around the clock.

Five years before Denny's became a public company, Jerome Richardson and Charles Bradshaw entered the restaurant business; they bought the first Hardee's restaurant franchise in Spartanburg, South Carolina. The two men were drawn to the area in part because both of them attended Wofford College there. Richardson had been a wide receiver for the Baltimore Colts in 1959, the year he helped to win an NFL championship against the New York Giants. He took his NFL bonus check—$4,600—and invested in the unheard-of idea of a hamburger restaurant franchise. That franchise was Hardee's, and by the time I joined the company, we owned 600 Hardee's franchise restaurants.

The two men had been teammates on their college football team, but their partnership off the field was a little riskier—they knew almost nothing about what they were doing. Richardson once said in an interview: "We didn't know how to balance a checkbook. We didn't know anything about bookkeeping." But he added that many people were eager to support the two of them as they worked to make a go of their hamburger restaurant.

"Many (people) were not necessarily coming in because it was a 15-cent hamburger. They were coming in because they were trying to help us be successful," Richardson would say later. "The community had to be patient. We just had all kinds of problems." In spite of those problems—everything from frozen milk shake machines to exploding soda machines—the two men did very well with that initial franchise, growing it into Spartan Food Systems, which went public in 1969.

By 1979, Richardson and Bradshaw's company was acquired by TransWorld Corporation, a company whose holdings included investments as varied as Hilton International, Canteen Corporation, and TransWorld Airlines. Richardson stayed on after the acquisition and continued to run the division he'd built from scratch, even as more changes continued to alter the corporation's ever more complex identity.

By 1986, TransWorld Corporation had spun off many of its earlier non–food-related investments, liquidated its old stock, and reformed itself as TW Services. Richardson's partner, Bradshaw, said to have been dissatisfied with the company's direction, quietly withdrew from the picture. The following year, 1987, TW Services purchased both Denny's restaurants and El Pollo Loco, a chain of grilled-chicken restaurants, and Richardson became president of the food service company. Its headquarters, once in New Jersey, were relocated to Spartanburg.

By 1993, we were known as Flagstar Companies, Inc. (At that time, Flagstar was the largest publicly held company based in South Carolina—today we are the third largest.) It had sales of almost $4 billion in fiscal 1993; the company at the time employed more than 100,000 people, 11,000 of them in South Carolina, and nearly 2,000 of those people lived and worked in Spartanburg.

Shockwave

Rob Barrett, our assistant general counsel, was one of those who lived in Spartanburg. A native of the town, Barrett had joined Flagstar in May 1991. He was eager to work for a national company without having to leave home, and Flagstar's recent relocation and consolidation made that possible. But in his wildest dreams, he never imagined in a little more than six months after joining the company, he'd be up to his neck in the ugliest kind of litigation.

In the early 1990s, individuals in several California communities had begun to complain about the treatment they said they'd received at Denny's restaurants. In reaction to some of those initial claims, at least two groups of lawyers— Saperstein, Mayeda, Larkin, and Goldstein, as well as the public-interest law firm of the Santa Clara County Bar Foundation, both in San Jose—had begun to compile complaints, statements, and other documentation that purported to prove Denny's racist practices. In addition, the U.S. Department of Justice had begun to look into charges that Denny's showed a pattern of discrimination against its customers who were people of color.

In educating myself about the tortured history of Denny's and discrimination, I learned that as early as January of 1992, my predecessor, Flagstar chairman Jerry Richardson, began talking with members of the local NAACP to discover how he and the Denny's team might respond to the challenge of diversifying the company he loved and in which he had invested so much. In time, those early meetings with the local branch of the NAACP led to higher-level meetings with national-level representatives of the NAACP.

Fred H. Rasheed, then head of the NAACP's economic development division, recalls vividly some of the early meetings. "Those first meetings were with Jerry Richardson and three or four of his staff people in Spartanburg," Rasheed remembered. "The meeting got a little heated between Richardson and Dr. [William] Gibson, the NAACP board chairman.

"These were two very strong personalities, both South Carolinians and both somewhat combative. I could tell that Jerry kind of resented the tone of the comments Dr. Gibson made. There was no cursing, but it was loud.

"At one point, Jerry said, 'Perhaps we should end the meeting; I don't appreciate this!' It was almost a pretty short meeting. But I tried to cool the parties down. Basically, I said, 'Let's look at the bigger picture here, and put our personal feelings aside.' I think it ended on a positive note."

As Rasheed recalls the gathering, Richardson announced to the group that Denny's had just formed a diversity committee within the company that included at least two African-Americans. "Jerry said, 'I'd like representatives of the NAACP to meet with this group, and whatever their recommendations are, I'll take them under serious consideration.'"

In fact, the group's recommendation to the company was that Denny's pursue a fair share agreement with the NAACP, an agreement that set serious goals for the company in areas as varied as contracting with minority suppliers, developing minority-owned franchisees, and the number of people of color on our board of directors. The agreement would even address Denny's willingness to make a commitment to using African-American media and ad agencies in helping to communicate with black consumers.

A great deal of the tension Rasheed recalled in his meetings between Denny's representatives and NAACP representatives, I think, came from Jerry Richardson's horror at being considered a racist who ran a racist company.

"The suits were a crushing blow to him," said Paul Raether of Kohlberg Kravis Roberts & Co. (KKR), an investment group with a controlling interest in Flagstar. "He doesn't think of himself as a racist and would not condone discrimination against anybody. He felt personally offended by the claims made against Denny's."

It didn't help that once the charges by the Secret Service agents were made, one of the law firms—Saperstein, Mayeda—ran a series of ads targeted at minority populations, complete with toll-free numbers. The firm invited those who believed they had been discriminated against at any Denny's restaurant to contact the firm for information on possible litigation against the company. For Rob Barrett, our assistant general counsel, the convergence of so many negative stories about the alleged discriminatory practices of his company were nightmarish.

"We were running around like you can't believe," he recalled. "We began to get just hundreds of calls here. There were customers [who] were supportive; there were those who were critical. There were many customers who wanted us to know about their issues and experiences in our restaurants. We were feeling under siege at that stage of the game."

Rob also recalls feeling somewhat relieved when the U.S. Department of Justice announced its original intention to probe charges of discrimination. It was his thinking that "they [Justice] will see that there was no intentional policy to discriminate. No one in this building was issuing edicts to the field about how to mistreat customers."

But the reality of what the Department of Justice would find was quite different from Rob's optimistic expectations. Rob recalls the department saying nothing for months. "They asked us for information; we gave the information willingly. Then we had a period of time where there was no response and—boom!—the letter from Justice comes in October and we're just floored. We were absolutely floored."

The letter said, according to Rob, that the Department of Justice believed there was "evidence of a pattern and practice of intentional discrimination in a place of public accommodation, and you either enter into a consent decree or we're going to sue you. You could have knocked me over with a feather, you know; there was no wind in me. It just wasn't the way we viewed it was going to go. I thought, 'Our government's involved; they'll see the truth of this.'"

On the same day that those six Secret Service agents claimed to encounter such terrific difficulties getting breakfast, attorneys for Denny's entered into a consent decree in California resolving the claims of the Department of Justice. What exactly is a consent decree? It is a court order in which parties to a settlement state all the terms of their agreement. Somewhere along the line, one group or the other decides not to spend enormous amounts of time and money tied up in court for months, possibly years, as rulings are appealed again and again. Instead, the two sides come up with an agreement about ways to remedy the situation, rather than risking the uncertainty of a trial.

Though Denny's tried hard not to settle, the company ended up paying $54 million to settle the class-action suits, including $8 million in attorney's fees, when Richardson finally signed off on the case in 1994. The consent decree that we signed concerning the treatment of the Secret Service agents in Annapolis conformed with an amended version of the consent decree signed on April 1, 1993, so that the two documents would not conflict.

No one at Flagstar really believed there was a company-wide conspiracy to demean and humiliate customers of color. No one at the company really believed there was an organized desire to deny service to anyone on the basis of race. But the consent decree, the $54 million settlement that resulted from it, the host of promises we had to make in order to fulfill the requirements of that decree—all these events created a climate of self-examination throughout the ranks. To the credit of my predecessors, they had begun to address some of the issues raised by customer claims even before the Justice Department got involved. But it would take the focus and intentionality that came with the pressure—and yes, the shame—of a consent decree to really make us understand how easy it was for any company, even with the best intentions in the world, to end up creating a climate that allowed people to be treated in a way that was biased and unfair. Even before I arrived, Flagstar knew there was a lot to learn. The question was: Could we learn it in time to save the company and its reputation?

My Introduction to Denny's

So—how did I find myself in Spartanburg, South Carolina, knee-deep in lawsuits and bad publicity? Good question. I was minding my business at Burger King headquarters in Miami, where I'd been since 1991, when Barry Gibbons, the company's chairman and chief executive officer, hired me. I'd been brought in as president of Burger King's company-owned stores. The chain's operations and sales were my responsibility. But when I think back on it, I can see that my work at Burger King, as well as in other positions I've held, did a good job of preparing me for the massive work I would face at Advantica.

I started selling suits at the Bon Marché in Seattle, right out of college, and over time, marketing became my area of expertise. I had a chance to work in businesses as varied as Target Stores and B. Dalton Booksellers. But it wasn't until I got to Revco (now CVS), the number two drugstore chain in the country, that I had an opportunity to really exercise the skills I'd been developing throughout my retailing career. Revco was my first turnaround experience; deep into bankruptcy because of the combination of over-expansion and a shifting marketplace for retail drugs for a time, Revco was a wonderful challenge for me. But once our team had helped the drug company move toward exiting bankruptcy, it became clear that it was time for me to move on. We sold our house, sold our car, and my wife, Lyn, and our two sons lived for a while in a two-bedroom apartment in Cleveland, Ohio, until Gibbons at Burger King hired me.

I'd had a great time at Burger King, working with Gibbons as well as the company's founder, Jim McLamore. I certainly didn't have any particular plans to leave Miami, and even if I had, there was never a thought in my mind that I wanted to live in Spartanburg, South Carolina. I'm not sure I knew where it was! But that was before my courtship with KKR, the leveraged buyout firm.

KKR had held a controlling financial interest in Flagstar since late 1992, and part of the deal included several seats on the company's board of directors. What I couldn't have known was that because Flagstar's debt continued to be a problem, KKR was looking for leadership from someone who'd had experience in turning around troubled companies. One of KKR's general partners, Paul Raether, had taken the lead in the firm's search for a new executive for Flagstar. Paul said they'd heard about me and about my earlier turnaround work, then used an executive search firm, Spencer Stuart, where my name also surfaced. In addition, Paul tells me, they'd asked around about me and checked into my background. I guess they liked what they saw, because while I was vacationing in Vail, Colorado, I got a call one afternoon from Paul, also in Vail, who asked: "Would you like to come over and have a drink with Henry Kravis at his house?"

It's not unusual to get calls from executive recruiters once you've been in this business for a while, and as I said, I didn't have any interest in leaving Burger King. It's very different, however, and very flattering, to get a call from KKR with an offer of drinks with Henry Kravis. I wouldn't be telling the truth if I didn't admit to a certain amount of uneasiness. KKR is probably best known for their takeover of RJR Nabisco, the subject of articles, books, and movies, including the best-selling book *Barbarians at the Gate: The Fall of RJR Nabisco*. I wasn't really sure they were people with whom I wanted to work. At the same time, what was the harm in a drink? So I agreed, and asked if Lyn could come along.

I wanted Lyn to be with me because in many ways, she's more intuitive than I am. In fact, Lyn interviewed Henry, asking about the company, its goals, the way KKR conducted its business. Henry knew she was doing the interviewing, too. After a while, we said our good-byes, and Lyn and I went to dinner.

Lyn liked Henry Kravis, and she liked his answers to her inquiries. "They sound like people with a lot of integrity," she said, and I felt the same way. We agreed that if they continued to pursue me, I would take them seriously. That wasn't so hard. The company they wanted me to run was in the midst of incredible challenges, both financially and socially. Financially, Flagstar was a struggling company. As our negotiations progressed, I had sense enough to ask how much struggle we were talking about.

How the Numbers Crunched Denny's

The company had carried a crushing debt load since 1989, as a result of a hostile takeover by the private equity firm of Gollust, Tierney & Oliver, or GTO. The company paid the holders of 30 million shares of the company—which up until then had been called TW Services Inc.—$34 for each share, which came either in cash or in some combination of cash and shares in the new company, which was TW Holdings, Inc.

Our many name changes have been difficult to track, so a brief summary here might be in order: The company was TW Holdings until KKR decided to rescue it in 1992 by investing $300 million of equity to restructure its debt. This new equity investment meant that KKR took effective control of the company. The following year, the company had a new name—Flagstar. That would be the company's name for the next five years, when it was discharged from a Chapter 11 bankruptcy in 1998. At that time, the company again took a new name for its new situation—Advantica, as we are now known. So Denny's has had a parent company with three different names in the 1990s: TW Holdings, Flagstar, and Advantica.

I learned from KKR that to finance the purchase of so much TW Services stock, it employed several strategies, including selling some unwanted assets and mortgaging many of its restaurant properties. Not least of all, TW had to go out and convince its lenders that it could afford to pay back the debt it had taken on to pay for that stock. To do this, management told those lenders that it expected the cash flow from the company's various business units—Denny's, the Hardee's franchises, and Canteen Corporation, a contract food service division, were the most important at the time—to be strong enough in coming years to cover the debt payments. Making that happen was not impossible, but it was difficult. Because of the highly leveraged position of the company, TW had been forced to borrow money at high rates of interest—between 10% and 17%. In addition, the company also had to pay the lenders significant up-front fees to complete these transactions. So by the early 1990s, TW faced staggering interest payments.

That, in turn, hindered its ability to use the cash flow it did have for business purposes like marketing expenses, remodeling restaurants, and the other day-to-day expenditures that would draw in more customers. Instead, cash flow had to be used to pay off interest charges. And without money to plow back into operations, TW could not expand its various businesses and generate the cash flow it needed to cover the interest charges on its debt.

The result of these complex transactions? The company went from having about $1 billion of borrowed money on its balance sheet in 1988 to having more than $2.4 billion by the end of 1989. If TW Holdings had made huge profits in the years immediately after the buyout, or even moderate profits, this might not have been a problem. But times had become rougher. The economy that looked so rosy in 1987, and even so-so in 1989, had turned decidedly sluggish and sour by 1990 and 1991. The nation was going into recession and TW's divisions were feeling the fallout from the weak economy. All in all, revenues in the recession of 1991 didn't meet the forecasts of two years earlier, leaving less cash on hand to cover interest costs. TW was in serious trouble by the time KKR came around and decided that with an equity infusion, the restructuring of the company's debt to cut interest costs, and the right management, TW would make a good investment.

During our negotiations, I asked KKR to show me the books, to talk to me about the numbers, to let me know how this company was doing financially. In truth, the situation at Flagstar by 1993 was still pretty bad. The recession was just starting to end, but the company was still feeling some pressure. The number of Flagstar company owned and operated restaurants had begun to decline in 1994 as the number of franchise operations began rising. They hadn't yet made any great cutbacks in those units Flagstar actually owned, though that was a strategy I would later embrace. Franchising became an important growth strategy and we began to aggressively expand our franchise operations.

I also saw that Flagstar had written off assets of $1.5 billion in 1993, principally, goodwill and other intangible assets acquired in the 1989 transaction. What the write-off represented was simply more fallout from the 1989 leveraged buyout. Typically, in deals like that, the buyers pay a premium over the value of the tangible assets of the company. Unfortunately, due to the recession, this premium wasn't worth much at all. When you see a company take action like that, you have to admire their willingness to take the hard steps and admit to their misjudgment. When you consider the mammoth deals being done in American business these days, $1.5 billion doesn't sound like a great deal of money. But at that time, it was a substantial sum for Flagstar to write off.

Everything listed on Flagstar's books just wasn't as valuable as the company wanted to think. Or to put it another way, the original price paid for the company's stock in 1989 was too high. That was not readily apparent when the deal happened. But by 1993 it was, so writing off the assets meant that shareholders were ready to admit that and absorb the loss—a net loss of $40 a share.

Indeed the entire company was going through a significant restructuring in 1993 and 1994. Layers and layers of middle management were being eliminated, though many restaurant managers ended up with more control over their restaurants than before, as the organizational chart at Flagstar essentially became flatter. It was clear, in short, that KKR had every intention of fighting to keep its $300 million investment. I knew that KKR as a group was recognized for its prowess in picking companies in which to invest; there was no reason to believe that they would pump $300 million cash into a bottomless pit.

It was clear that an assessment of Flagstar's financial condition could have gone either way. But what was not very clear, until at least a year after I joined Flagstar, was that Hardee's would turn out to be the weak link in the chain of companies that we operated. As time went on, we would decide to sell many of our businesses. Since I have come aboard, we have sold Quincy's Family Steakhouse, a 180-unit chain of restaurants in the southeast, as well as several food service businesses, so that we could concentrate on our restaurant businesses. To bolster our presence in the nation's largest market, California, we bought two chains there in 1996: Coco's, a chain of bakery restaurants with 481 units, both company and franchise owned, and Carrows, a moderately priced chain of family restaurants. At the end of 1998, Carrows had 149 units, about 85% of which are company owned. Little did I know, when I was preparing to run Flagstar, that Hardee's, which we would eventually sell, would prove such a difficult and time-consuming situation.

We owned 600 Hardee's franchises, and as we continued to work with the franchisor, we felt the brand was woefully mismanaged. We believed Imasco, the Canadian company that owned Hardee's, had not put together a very good team. In our judgment, their marketing programs were neither innovative nor creative, and all of the Hardee's franchisees were anxious for the parent company to create new products, something difficult to do at the local level.

Later on, as Paul Raether remembers, we tried to sue Hardee's. Technically, we couldn't sue under our franchise agreement—only go to arbitration—so we filed a demand for arbitration to get their attention. We asked for a huge amount of damages, something like $500 million; failing that, we wanted those 600 units to be removed from the Hardee's system. We figured that if we could convert them to Denny's or Quincy's or any of the brands under our control, we would have a better shot at making them work than if we left them in a system that was not performing. That was a strategic move on our part. We knew we couldn't get the money, or get rid of the arbitrators, but we were paying Imasco about $25 million in annual royalties and getting little in return. Finally, in 1998, we sold our Hardee's restaurants to CKE Restaurants, who had acquired the Hardee's brand from Imasco.

As involved as my personal examination of the company must seem, it was important—and not just for the obvious reasons. True, I've built my reputation on turnarounds, as someone who can go into a financially troubled company and lead it back to health. To do that, I had to know in some detail just how much trouble we were talking about. But even more important, I knew Flagstar's troubles weren't just financial. The legacy of accusations against the company and the lack of faith in our good intentions had a cost to the company that could not be measured in just dollars and cents.

More Due Diligence

As I continued looking into Flagstar, I realized that everything I knew about the company's racial problems I'd gathered from reading, notably, the Sunday *New York Times Magazine*. I was aware of the settlement of the class-action lawsuit for $54 million. But there were other things that it took more time for me to understand. I realize now that there were significant numbers of African-Americans and others who claimed that my predecessor only saw the light and entered into the NAACP fair share agreement in response to threatened protests by civil rights leaders. Some of those people also believed that because Richardson was in pursuit of an NFL franchise (which he later won), he was more sensitive to criticism for fear that the continuing publicity about charges of racism would jeopardize his chance at the franchise he sought. In truth, I happen to think that neither event had much to do with Richardson's eventual commitments to both the consent decrees and the fair-share agreement. I simply think that he finally "got it"—though not without a little help from the company's board of directors, which by this time was run by the people from KKR.

It was the KKR board that agreed to settle the suits against the company before my arrival here. From talking to those board members informally and in getting to know them, it's my belief that they looked at it as cheaper than litigation. As I said earlier, Flagstar was not in the best financial shape at the time; I imagined they thought, "We can't risk $54 million turning into $100 million." I also think that KKR settled because they're the kind of people who would never tolerate discrimination.

We discussed this issue during the process of hiring me. I was set to meet with the board. Dr. Vera King Farris, the first African-American on the board, made it a point of asking several direct questions about whether I would take seriously the company's commitment to its fair share agreement. It was clear that she wanted to feel comfortable about my intentions before signing off on my appointment as CEO.

I can remember being pretty nervous in the face of her questioning. She asked me, essentially, "Where is your heart?" when it comes to this issue. Vera is a smart and sensitive woman who wanted to make sure I wasn't just mouthing words. To this day, I'm not sure I answered her questions directly, but I did tell her that the Reverend Willie Barrow, co-chair of Rainbow-PUSH Coalition (formerly Operation PUSH), was a close friend of mine. "I worked with [the] Reverend Barrow for four years on these kinds of issues," I told her. "If you want, just call her." Hearing that seemed to make Vera more comfortable with me.

It was through some early exposure to accusations of racial discrimination in my time at Burger King, as well as some practice in how to handle them, that I came to know the Reverend Barrow. For some time, there had been lawsuits and threatened boycotts involving African-American franchisees and the lack of support they felt from the company. Many of the franchisees were more vulnerable to slowing sales because they had borrowed so heavily to finance the purchases of their businesses. A lot of African-

Americans were encouraged to buy franchises in Burger King after complaints from Operation PUSH and the Reverend Jesse Jackson about the lack of black franchises. In fact, PUSH was one of those organizations that had threatened to boycott Burger King. To be frank, our relationships with Burger King franchisees—regardless of race—had been difficult for a while. But the issues raised by black franchisees were a particular problem. In working to resolve some of those issues, I came to know and respect the Reverend Barrow and her work, and I was glad to realize that the feeling was mutual.

So I was no stranger to the kind of difficulties Denny's seemed to be encountering. But in my mind, that had occurred in 1993 and was over and done. By the time Paul Raether, and Henry Kravis and the rest of the KKR group began courting me, I was under the impression that all those claims, all the trouble, was just so much unfortunate history.

When I joined the company, Henry Kravis personally came to every board meeting and sat through the entire session—and we had four or five of them a year. There was the need for that much involvement in the company as far as KKR was concerned; the company's reputation was at stake, too. It didn't help that we turned out to be the largest loss in the history of the KKR fund.

All of the work we've done here—at Denny's and throughout Advantica—has been so special to me, such an important chapter in my life. But I do wish I'd been a little more aware going in; I would have liked to know that the financial situation was far worse than I thought. For example, I didn't know at the time how fast or how far Hardee's would fall. And though I didn't know—couldn't know—

everything about the claims of discrimination, I gradually realized that I was more prepared than most people to lead in the work of changing the corporate culture.

Lessons in Life

One of the reasons I think I'm so conscious of how much difference the color of a person's skin can make is because of the way I grew up. My father was a general in the U.S. Army; I was born in Japan and lived in countries all over the world. My folks moved every two years until I was in high school. I know all that moving would drive some people crazy, but I loved it; it felt like a constant adventure.

The first five years of my childhood, I lived in Europe. I could speak fluent French by the time my family and I moved back to the United States. I think I could speak English, but not very well. Curiously enough, by the time I reached high school—we were living in Hawaii then—I had lost so much of the language that I actually flunked French in high school! I cannot tell a lie; it was Hawaii, after all, and I cared a lot more about the beach and about basketball than I did about French.

I'd been playing basketball since I was a kid. At one point, my dad was working at the Pentagon, and we were living in suburban Washington, D.C. I played ball every chance I got, and though I could have played closer to home, I spent most of my time on the basketball court with a group of African-American kids living in Washington. At first they teased me, since I was the only white kid on the court, but I loved the game. I wanted to play with the best, and they were the best. In a way, it borders on the stereotypical—this image of the one white guy playing a sport

that's considered "black." But the truth is more compli-
cated: First, I've always loved basketball. Second, we still
live in a society in which sports provide a rare opportunity
for whites and people of color to be together as peers.

I kept playing ball when we moved to Hawaii, too. In
fact, I made all-state in high school. Just like in Japan, just
like on the ball courts in D.C., living in Hawaii also meant
being the only white guy around. So I knew what it was like
to be a minority, or the only one.

I have also seen more than I wanted to about the
demeaning ways in which people treat one another because
of race. I'll never forget going to visit my father when I was
in college and he was in Charleston, South Carolina. He
was commandant of cadets at the Citadel back in the late
1960s and I was a freshman in college. I can remember sitting down next to my dad when he was having a haircut.
The man next to him was having his shoes shined by an
African-American. After he finished the shoes, the black
man began reading the newspaper. Then a white man came
in, sat down, grabbed the paper, and said, 'You can have it
back when I'm done with it.' When he was finished, he
threw the paper back on the floor. I thought to myself, "Oh,
my goodness." It's bothered me all these years to think
about that man's contempt for another human being.

I've learned some lessons in my working life, too, about
the importance of dignity and simple respect when it comes
to the lives of workers. I first learned the reality of the
restaurant business bit by bit at Burger King. Since I'm not
from this industry originally, my first week on the job at
Burger King I went to work in one of the restaurants as an
hourly employee. No one knew who I was. Even though I
joined the company as president of what was then called

the company stores (before I became CEO), that first week I still went to work every day cleaning tables and restrooms. I befriended many of the hourly employees; they were mostly Hispanic women, and I found that many had been there 10 or 12 years—something incredibly rare in the fast-food business. These women would change their clothes from the Burger King uniform to another fast-food uniform and go and work another shift. They were working 16 hours a day just to survive.

It was really hard to take, watching them work like that. But I learned why these women stayed at that restaurant for years. They were getting basically the same pay as the rest of the people in the other Burger King restaurants, where employee turnover was much greater. But their manager found ways to celebrate their birthdays; he found ways to say something nice to them after every shift. It was the human side of how they were treated that made a difference to them, that made them stay. That's why the restaurant operated better—more long-term employees worked there.

Long after I left that restaurant as an hourly worker, I would talk to our restaurant managers. I tried to explain that it wasn't just about the financial part at the end of the day, though that really did matter. Yes, you do have to get somewhere close to solving the problem of how employees can financially survive. But you also must try to get your arms around the fact that people want to be patted on the back. They want to be appreciated. Now when I talk to restaurant managers, I remember the lessons learned from my week as part of the restaurant crew. And I know now, when I go to a restaurant, not to just walk around, say, "It looks fine," and leave. I go back in the kitchen. I say hi and thanks, and I listen to them, because I know how much they do.

Meeting those women, working with them, helped remind me of the times in my own life when I was struggling. As an educated white man in American society, I realize there were never times in my life when I had to endure the same kind of uncertainty those hourly workers did. There is a buffer that comes with being white and male in America that can often shield you from the worst consequences. It's not that we white men never have a hard time, but the odds are stacked in our favor.

More than one of my friends asked me why I would leave Burger King to go to a place like Denny's. I'm good friends with a guy who is in the advertising business—Stedman Graham. I think I've known him for about 8 years. I was the keynote speaker in Miami a few years ago at a meeting of the National Urban League, just after coming to Flagstar— I spoke before a huge audience. Stedman came up to me afterward and said, "What are you doing over there? You've got your work cut out for you." But he knew me, and I think he knew there was some hope for change.

It's important to understand we were fighting a war on two fronts here when I arrived at Flagstar. There was the attempt to create a racially inclusive business that could attract customers of all races and earn the respect of the American dining public. At the same time, I had a chance to turn around a company mired in debt, a company uncertain about the fate of several divisions in which thousands of employees worked, a company burdened with interest expenses that drained its ability to grow.

Though I didn't know it at the time, our only way out would be to declare bankruptcy. By going into chapter 11, we bought the time we needed to restructure the company's finances in a rational way while we decided, without the creditors knocking at the door, what our strategy would be for the company in the long term. That meant what to keep and what to sell, and how to do it all so that we never, ever violated the principles of racial inclusion and diversity in which this company had come to believe.

On a very practical level, the job did offer my family an opportunity for a different quality of life. The move would eventually give my wife an opportunity to build our home in Greenville, South Carolina, not far from Advantica headquarters; our relocation provided her with a creative outlet that she really enjoyed. We found many benefits to living in a smaller community with a slower pace and a better quality of life. For me, though, the big appeal was the challenge that Denny's and Flagstar represented. Hard as I knew it would be, I knew this would be the biggest and most exciting challenge of my career.

CHAPTER

4

Beginning Again

On the morning of February 5, 1995, I arrived at the corporate offices of Flagstar in downtown Spartanburg. It was a rainy, miserable day, but even in the mist and downpour, our headquarters is hard to miss—ours is the tallest building and office complex in town. When my predecessor, Jerry Richardson, built the 16-story building in 1989, I believed he hoped to anchor a forthcoming renaissance in downtown Spartanburg, an ambition that was gradually coming to fruition by the time I arrived.

The very history of Flagstar seemed to surround me as I entered the sand-colored tower and walked to the elevators. More than 70,000 people worked at Flagstar when I came to take charge there, 2,000 of them in Spartanburg, including 600 management and support staff in our corporate headquarters. In large measure, all those people were my responsibility now.

I thought about how imposing the building looked, and how much work lay ahead. My executive assistant, Dory Djerf, had joined me the previous day in our new offices. We spent the quiet Sunday getting organized for the mission ahead, figuring out which office arrangements might work best and otherwise creating our own space. We'd made a good start, so on this Monday morning, I needed only to wait for the elevator that would take me to the sixteenth floor. I used my key card, an electronic device, to gain entry to the floor. It was the only part of this massive beige complex completely inaccessible to the rest of the employees.

I exited the elevator and walked down the starkly beautiful corridor, designed with bird's-eye maple and chrome fixtures. At one point in my walk down the hall, the wall became a bank of windows, looking out over Spartanburg, a town of 45,721 people (at least in 1994). On my right, I could look through the panels of glass into the futuristic executive conference room, complete with a massive boardroom table and matching chairs. It was a room, a setting, much more formal than I usually am.

At the end of the hall I saw my office, and before it, the desk where Dory would sit. We had already learned that not only were employees unable to access the executive floor, but that the hallways, the conference rooms, and the offices were all equipped with surveillance cameras, along with a bank of monitors at what would become Dory's desk. Our floor was representative of the entire building—soaring, elegant, subdued, and very formal—perhaps a little too formal for me. It was a far cry from the playful atmosphere of Burger King headquarters, complete with its crayon colors and flying hamburgers.

For Denny's and for all of our restaurants, the task was enormous, but painfully clear, and on that dreary day, I wondered very briefly what I'd walked into. This is a service business, after all, and our success depended—then and now—on making customers feel satisfied with the food we serve and the way we serve it. Most of all, we need to make sure that customers want to come back. The charges of discrimination and disrespect had damaged our image to near fatal levels. Our willingness to settle the claims and to commit to a program of change was only the start of our efforts to reassure our customers and reestablish some level of trust that we might later be able to build upon.

Even before we could start that, and all the while we were engaged in that process, however, I needed to be the standard-bearer. Leadership begins at the top, and I was determined to lead Flagstar away from the perception of being a poster child for bigotry and toward being the most inclusive, progressive company in America. Of course, I had great business reasons for doing it. Our owners at KKR wanted this situation to be fully resolved; our employees wanted to stop explaining why they worked at a company with a reputation like ours; stockholders wanted us to get on with the business of serving good food at fair value.

But I had my own personal reasons for wanting to turn Flagstar around, both financially and socially. I wanted to do it because it was the right thing to do. I had spent my life growing up with people from all over the world. I had learned from personal experience how it felt to be in the minority, how it felt when people made assumptions about you without knowing anything about you—as a teenager, for example, when I was the only white kid playing basketball with black kids. And I also knew how it felt to be part of a team, once people got to know you and what you were capable of doing. It was a feeling I wanted to create at Advantica, just as I had helped to do at Burger King. I knew I couldn't do it by myself. But in the end, it was my responsibility to lead a company we could all be proud to work for, and I was ready to get started.

Making Things Clear

That first week, we had a lot of meetings. But the most important meeting, I think, occurred in the company auditorium. We had gathered there so that I could introduce myself, so that I could talk about the company, and so that I could talk about my dreams for turning things around, both in terms of our image and in terms of our bottom line. I talked about several things in that first meeting, but there are two things I remember most.

The first thing I remember telling everyone was that it was a new day here at Denny's. I knew that they'd been through a lot, that the negative attention focused on the company was sapping their energy and their pride in their work. But I told them that we were going to transform every part of this company—not just Denny's but all of Flagstar. I told them that the most important thing we could do right now was to be good to each other, and to be good to the customer. That was important to me, and it's something I still say every chance I get. I wanted them to know, too, that there was no chance that discrimination of any kind would be tolerated in any way in any part of this company. It was the first chance to say publicly what I would come to say thousands of times throughout the process of changing the company: "If you discriminate, we will fire you. Period." No one would ever be able to say they didn't know.

The other thing I wanted to do was subtler, I think. Though our building looks imposing, and though in most ways, Flagstar was organized much as any corporate entity might be, I wanted to send a clear signal with my arrival. I chose to start with the question of access—most particularly, access to me and to the sixteenth floor. Frankly, I told them that it was lonely up there, with only four people on the entire sixteenth floor: Dory, me, the chief financial officer, and his assistant. I told them all that they were welcome to talk to me about the changes we were making, and Dory and I said they were welcome to come up and visit us. People who work for you at headquarters ought to be able to see where you do your job. They ought to know that they have access to top management in the company if they have something on their mind. So we opened the top floors, and our doors.

I asked Dory to have the engineers reprogram the card key readers, so that everyone's cards worked on every floor of the building. Then, I began to meet with members of the support staff and other employees who worked at our headquarters, telling them that this was a company with open doors and—I hoped—open minds and hearts as well. It might seem small, but I think it sent a powerful signal.

I had learned at Burger King to break up some of the hierarchical structure that keeps people from knowing each other and working well together. The people in our corporate headquarters were so amazed at this gesture that Dory and I ended up giving tours of the executive floors, including the well-designed boardroom and some pretty impressive views of a blossoming Spartanburg. Employees visited our floors at regular intervals for about four months.

I wanted to send another message, too—that we were all in this together, executives and servers, managers and stake-holders. The financial package I received for coming to Flagstar was a generous one, including a guaranteed first-year bonus of $500,000. Later that year, we put that bonus to good use by placing it in a pool for managers of our Hardee's restaurant unit, which was one of our most finan-cially troubled chains. The idea was to reward those man-agers whose sales surpassed earlier sales numbers. There were about 2,000 of these managers—both general man-agers and assistant managers. Most managers in the pool received a bonus, and though it was small, it was my way of saying how much I appreciated the effort they'd been mak-ing under very difficult circumstances.

The bonus for me was a great gesture, and one I appreci-ated. But I didn't want to take the money. After all, there were shareholders who had paid good money for our stock—$12 to $15 a share at one point. But when I arrived, those same shares were worth as little as $3.50. We weren't going to be able to give bonuses to our officers either, not with the way things were going for us financially. I just didn't think it was right. I felt the same way about accept-ing a raise the following year. To my mind, there wasn't any point in taking a raise, given the circumstances we were in. It's true, I make a lot more money than any of our 70,000 workers, but if Flagstar didn't get turned around—in more ways than one—not one of us would make a dime. It was way too early to tell whether the people in place in all our units would be the right team for this job, but for that moment, I wanted to act as if they were. I wanted them to know that our turnaround, when it came, would depend on every one of us.

Within two weeks of my arrival, I decided it would be important to send another message—that I was taking seriously the notions of diversity and inclusion that I'd talked about my first week. I felt it was important for the company to honor Dr. Martin Luther King's birthday; he was a genuine American hero, as far as I was concerned, and deserved our recognition. So I declared the day a holiday at the headquarters. I didn't take away any of the existing holiday schedule, either, in the way that some companies do. I just added a day.

Well, I got about two dozen angry and confused e-mail messages from Flagstar employees about the addition of the holiday. Some folks wanted to know why we had to take that particular day off; others wanted to know why it wouldn't make more sense to give an extra day off when they felt they could use it—nearer to Christmas, for example. Here are just a few excerpts:

- "The overall impression I have been getting for several months ... has been very negative concerning the fact the company is paying more attention to the outcries of a few and the feelings and beliefs of the majority are getting stepped on or ignored. ... I am getting cheated in order to appease a strong, intimidating minority percentage of people."

- "Only a small percentage of employees celebrate Dr. King's birthday, but a great majority celebrate Christmas and Easter. These holidays are in honor of Jesus Christ and I think it is a disgrace for this company to put the importance of any man's birthday before Jesus, no matter who he is."

- "Why not President's Day??? How can you justify one and not the other, when in all reality President's Day is part of our American heritage regardless of your culture or religious beliefs, and that day has been recognized/observed/celebrated long before there ever was a Martin Luther King Day?"

I was a bit surprised, a bit upset that there were people who still couldn't understand the importance of someone like Dr. King. So at one point, I spoke at a support center meeting—our largest gathering of headquarters employees—about why we were honoring this day. I wasn't angry about the opposition I got; the larger goal was to communicate that from now on, things here would be different.

The Right to Know

I tried to bring the same directness and transparency to information about our financial restructuring process. Even while we were learning more each day about how to make our company more representative of our customers—and our country—we were faced with serious financial difficulties. We needed to restructure our massive debt, and that meant working things out in federal bankruptcy court. In a company as beleaguered as ours, that was one more piece of bad news.

That's one reason I believe so strongly in communicating with our people. Too many companies, whenever they reach some level of difficulty, keep the bad news isolated among a few top executives. That's usually a mistake. There are few secrets in a company, and even if there were, most people aren't stupid. Employees know when things aren't going well, and if you don't give them information, they're likely to be even more anxious. That wouldn't be good for business, because we needed to have everyone's full attention on their respective tasks as we worked on creating an inclusive company.

So as we embarked on our work with our bondholders, with the banks and the lawyers and the Securities and Exchange Commission, it was very important for me to let our employees know how hard we were working to create a new beginning for us here as well.

Throughout 1997, as we bargained and consulted and negotiated for the company's new financial start, I wanted very much to keep in touch. With the assistance of members of our communications and corporate relations teams, I communicated widely and often with our employees, through meetings, letters, e-mails, and even voice mail, when that made sense.

In late January of that year, I wrote to everyone to announce our hiring of Donaldson, Lufkin & Jenrette to help us structure a long-term solution to the $2.2 billion of debt we had incurred since the company's 1989 leveraged buyout. I was clear with everyone that we didn't need cash, that we had credit with major banks, and that before interest payments, all of our businesses were operating at a profit.

It was especially important to me, however, to speak as directly as I could to the anxieties of these people who depended on us to do well. As I wrote:

> During this period, there may be a lot of rumor and speculation about what this does or does not mean and what will or will not happen. I urge you not to be distracted by what you may hear or read. As soon as there is news to report, you have my word that I will share it with you. The one thing you can do is continue to do your best, which I know you

will. I pledge to you that I will provide the best leadership I possibly can during this period. ... Thank you, once again, for everything you do each and every day for our customers and fellow employees. I truly appreciate it.

I made it a point, in this letter, and in every one that followed, to invite our people to ask questions. We included the e-mail address for Stephen Wood, our executive vice president of human resources and corporate affairs, since he would act as our point person on specifics. For those of our employees in the restaurants without access to corporate e-mail, we sent the same letters and memos to each site, to be placed on the employee bulletin boards.

By March, we had reached an agreement in principle with our largest class of debtholders, those holding senior subordinated debentures. Though we were still working out details and I couldn't give out more specific information, I wanted to honor my promise to keep employees informed. We attached for distribution the press release that was issued the same day and we scheduled two meetings with employees in Spartanburg for the following week. By that time, more of the details would be settled and those of us working on the deal would be available to answer questions. Most important, I reemphasized the bottom-line issues for our workers: first, that the restructuring wouldn't affect the day-to-day operation of the restaurant units, and second, that we had no reason to believe that we'd have to lay off anyone because of our restructuring work.

By May, we were well on our way to approval of our financial restructuring plan. It was important for all of us to greet this forthcoming reorganization as the new beginning that it was. That's part of what I wrote to all our employees in the letter I sent to everyone, and I added this:

To signal a break with the past and reflect the new, positive direction associated with our new company, we have decided to change our parent company's name. We are evaluating a number of possibilities for the best name to identify us as a successful company that operates several restaurant brands. Our new name will be of particular importance as we issue new stock and attract new investors to our company.

Many of our employees, in fact, sent us suggestions on possible names for the new company—dozens of suggestions that we couldn't really use, largely because they were already trademarked. Several of our workers wanted to use the words "advantage," or "America" in the new name. That was clearly impossible, but we could use elements of those cherished terms to create a new name for our new company. That's how Advantica got its name—one of the strongest messages yet that everything here was changing.

CHAPTER

5

The Promises We Made

I knew that even before I arrived at Flagstar, the company attempted to make significant changes in the way it dealt with people of color at every point of contact. I believe that I've assembled an extraordinary team of professionals with a heartfelt commitment to transforming the company culture, making inclusiveness and diversity part of the way we do business. I also know, however, that some of the groundwork for our success was laid before my arrival.

Several things were foundational for the Denny's transformation. I wouldn't be truthful if I didn't admit that some of that groundwork was imposed upon us because of the consent decree. In addition, Flagstar signed an early fair share agreement with the NAACP shortly *before* we came to agreement with the U.S. Department of Justice and settled the two class-action lawsuits. Together, these two agreements provided all of us with both a wake-up call and a benchmark. For those among us who "didn't think we were that bad" or felt that the discrimination and bias we were charged with were simply isolated incidents, these two official agreements took us out of the realm of blame and into the realm of action. What became most important was not whether we were a racist company but whether we were as good as our word. Both of these documents included promises we made to other groups of people, but they also included promises we made to ourselves—and to the 1 million people we served each and every day. We promised to stay awake—awake to the ways we could continue to improve our business relationships with people of color, awake to the ways we could create opportunities for and partnerships with the diversity of people we serve. Most of all, we promised that, once awakened to all these possibilities, we would act on what we knew.

The Nuts and Bolts of Fairness

As I said earlier, a consent decree is a court order in which parties to a settlement state all the terms of their agreement (see Figure 5.1). Flagstar and the U.S. Department of Justice entered into an agreement to avoid the stream of litigation that several people and groups promised would follow our failure to sign such an agreement. A key point of the agreement is the restatement of current antidiscrimination law. These restatements were included, in spite of the fact that they are already on the books, because it was important for all of us to be reading from the same page.

In general terms, we state that our company and its employees will treat all customers equally well. In cases like this, however, generalities aren't good enough; neither the lawyers for the plaintiffs, nor those at the justice department, would have signed off on weakly worded documents that emphasized our desire to do better. It's the details that count, and the consent decree lays them all out, listing the 15 practices that must not be handled differently, in the decrees' words, "on the basis of race, color, or national origin."

Consent Decree Requirements

The Consent Decrees specifically forbid discrimination on the basis of race or color. Each of the requirements listed below applies to all people regardless of race, color, or national origin.

1. Everyone is entitled to the full and equal enjoyment of the goods, services, facilities, privileges, advantages, and accommodations of Denny's restaurants regardless of race, color, or national origin.

2. Do not deny service, or offer lesser service, to any person on the basis of race, color, or national origin.

3. Do not deny service, or offer less favorable terms of service to guests who are part of a group that includes African-Americans or other racial or ethnic minorities.

4. Do not require prepayment, cover, or minimum charge, added service charge, or require identification on the basis of race, color, or national origin as a condition for service.

5. Do not refuse to seat, take meal orders, or serve any guest on the basis of race, color, or national origin.

6. Do not require any guest to wait longer, or provide inferior services to any guest on the basis of race, color, or national origin.

7. Ensure that everyone receives properly cooked food, fit to eat.

8. Never make derogatory or inflammatory comments about any groups of people and never knowingly allow such comments to be made.

9. Do not make statements about any groups of people that would discourage a reasonable person from visiting Denny's.

10. Do not threaten to remove any guest by force on the basis of race, color, or national origin.

11. Do not segregate any guest within the restaurant on the basis of race, color, or national origin.

12. Do not implement different terms or conditions for any group of guests concerning any promotional offers, such as the "Grand Slam" offer, on the basis of race, color, or national origin.

13. Do not make, print, publish, or supervise production of any notice, statement, or advertisement regarding service or equal enjoyment of our restaurants that indicates an actual or intended preference, limitation, or discrimination of any group of guests.

14. Do not indicate to any person that service or enjoyment of our restaurants is not available when this is not true.

15. Never retaliate against any employee for opposing or reporting alleged discrimination in the service or treatment of guests.

NOTE: All employees regardless of their own race, color, or national origin are required to follow the requirements.

Figure 5.1 Denny's consent decree requirements.

It is a sad fact that though the vast majority of our employees are good and fair people, certain rules of common sense and decency still have to be spelled out. In this case, however, we were under legal obligation to spell them out. Detailing specifics of behavior—for example, the fact that Denny's cannot lie to anyone by telling him or her that a particular service is closed when it is, in fact, open—certainly would have taken care of the most egregious instances of racism.

Other segments of the consent decree were just as detailed. It was clear that Denny's management knew it would have to undertake some sort of advertising to let people know the company was making an attempt to change. Denny's also needed to reach out to minority customers who by then were so soured on the company that they might never have eaten at a Denny's again. We wanted to create ads that talked about our attitude as well as our food. How those ads were presented to the public, however, was a matter of great concern.

Not only did we have to make that advertising racially inclusive, we were told in great detail exactly how to measure the level of inclusion that would be necessary. Again, a simple "We'll do better" wouldn't cut the mustard. Thirty percent of the people in all newspaper ads and promotional materials had to be, as the decree put it, "identifiably" nonwhite, whereas at least 25% of the total number of folks in these ads and brochures and such had to be specifically African-American.

For our television ads, we even had to compute how long these nonwhite faces appeared on the screen. Let me quote from the decree:

African-American persons shall be principally featured as employees or customers a minimum of twenty-five percent of the time during which any employees or customers of Denny's are depicted. This percentage shall be computed by dividing the number of seconds each African-American person is depicted as a customer or employee in a television commercial by the number of seconds any person is depicted as a customer or employee in a television commercial.

The consent decrees defined several other ways for us to send a signal that Denny's had a commitment to fairness and equity. For example, we needed to publish in any promotional ads a nondiscrimination statement as follows:

We are committed to providing the best possible service to all customers regardless of race, color, creed, or national origin.

The nondiscrimination statement had to be in the same size type as the rest of the advertisement if only one size type was used in the ad. It could be printed in either of two sizes if two sizes of print were used; if three or more different sizes were used, it had to be at least in the next to smallest size of print.

Denny's was required to post signs in its restaurants saying that it would not discriminate against any customer on the basis of race, color, or national origin. Just any sign wouldn't do, though. Very specifically, the company agreed to make these signs with "dark letters at least one inch high on a contrasting background."

These were small things to do, but they were important foundational work. These gestures helped to create the climate for change on our part and sent a message to others that things were different than before. By 1994, everybody at Denny's was starting to get with the program, not just legally but emotionally as well. Still, there were several additional requirements under the consent decrees that Denny's had to undertake.

Ignorance Is Unacceptable

One of the most important of these additional requirements was that we had to notify, within 60 days, all of our franchisees about our participation in the consent decree. Fulfilling this notification requirement did mean we were not held legally responsible for mavericks—the sort of franchisees who had been told clearly what would be required at the new Denny's but decided they could ignore our directives. Although the fulfillment of the notice requirement enabled Denny's to avoid legal blame for the actions of a potential maverick, both Denny's top management and the Office of the Civil Rights Monitor, known to us then as the OCRM, did not condone or accept any ill treatment of customers by a maverick. The OCRM, established by the consent decree and headquartered in California, was the legal entity charged with making sure that Denny's complied with the consent decree. The civil rights monitor was empowered to send testers into Denny's restaurants and to receive and act on all complaints concerning the behavior at Denny's from anyone in the country. We were duty-bound to cooperate with any investigation the OCRM decided to carry out.

The franchisees were notified very early about the consent decree. Remember that the Annapolis incident happened just as the initial consent decree with the justice department was agreed on in northern California. Whatever internal communications were in existence—whether formal or informal—to make sure Denny's managers understood the company's commitment to issues of diversity and inclusion, they hadn't worked. So it was important that the restaurant managers be notified, both for their individual sakes and for the corporation's.

We had 60 days after the consent decree was signed to notify everybody at Denny's that there was going to be a new way of doing business under this consent decree. And everybody—managers and restaurant personnel—had to acknowledge in writing and send back a dated copy of a form that said that they read and understood our nondiscrimination policy, which read, in part:

> I understand the requirements of the Amended Decree and the non-discrimination policies and procedures, and recognize that my failure or refusal to adhere to them could result in possible sanctions against me by a court as well as disciplinary action, including termination of my employment, by my employer.

So everybody who worked for Denny's was indeed reading off the same page at last, and here was the proof—in black and white. There was no longer a question of what was and what was not acceptable behavior at Denny's.

The consent decree also said that the civil rights monitor was to conduct tests at Denny's, sending groups of testers posing as customers to measure fair treatment. By the end of 1999, more than 2,500 tests had been conducted by the OCRM at Denny's nationwide.

Do claims of discrimination still arise, even after these basic structures were put into place? Of course they do. But what we have here now that we didn't have before is a serious process of investigation, one modeled on the OCRM but certainly not tethered to that office.

Of course, the OCRM does not make its investigations public. Yet in one high-profile case, for example, a separate investigation was conducted by the local district attorney's office, which made public a report of its own.

The incident, which took place April 11, 1997 in Syracuse, New York, involved a group of Asian-American students. Some of them became involved in a brawl outside the local franchise Denny's restaurant when they believed white customers had entered the restaurant and were seated first, after the Asian-American students had been waiting for a table for a lengthy period.

This separate investigation by the Onondaga County district attorney's office concludes that it could find no evidence that Denny's servers, managers, or security guards had done anything to discriminate against the students. The Asian students were in a group of seven, and tables could not be found to accommodate them at that hour. Many nearby bars in the university neighborhood had just closed and the restaurant was extremely busy. The district attorney's staff—which was composed of a senior assistant district attorney, Lisa Marie Fletcher, and a senior investigator, Carol Sacco—said in response to the complaints of the Denny's participants:

> ...The restaurant was very crowded and unable to accommodate a large group at the time the students wanted to be seated. [The employees] all state that it is not unusual to wait 30 minutes or more for a table at that hour of the morning. Nothing from our interviews leads us to the conclusion that the students were discriminated against, or that they were ejected without cause.

As I've said, the OCRM performs its investigations confidentially, so we can't talk about the details of its findings. But this incident still points up to our many employees that complaints about service must be dealt with appropriately and quickly, or they become complaints about discriminatory treatment instead, even if there is no objective proof of that—and of course, we consider the district attorney's investigation here to be objective.

Employees of our company know when they arrive that we won't stand for discriminatory behavior of any kind. The consent decree mandates that those employees who joined the company after the consent decree took effect are instructed to sign the same notification as were employees who were already working there in May 1994. We agreed that they would be notified within seven days of hire. And if the OCRM found some instance in which it believed the consent decree had been violated, that office could hold up this notice, signed by the employee himself or herself, and find an individual guilty of civil rights violations.

The consent decree asked Denny's to make a major commitment to training. This was one issue that I had to grow into, quite honestly, because as I've said many times before, I remain ambivalent about training. Sometimes I think people simply need to be told to do the right thing. You give them a chance to do it; then, if they don't follow through, you fire them.

But for those people working here prior to my arrival, experience had taught them that one of the largest issues facing the company was the lack of a clear statement of expectation when dealing with customers of all races. They also had no direction in situations that could lead either to discrimination or the perception of discrimination—such as a restaurant employee who gives a customer change but puts it on the counter instead of in the customer's hand, as if touching the hand of someone black were something awful and to be avoided. That is the type of action that not only shows insensitivity to our customers but could lead to further lawsuits and to the company's running afoul of the consent decree.

So it was vital to train all our restaurant managers and give proof to the OCRM that this training in how to treat people was *real*. The OCRM had to approve exactly which videotapes we would show our employees and how and where we would show them. Who we had to show them to was pretty easy—everybody! Officers, division heads, servers, hosts, regional heads, managers, managers in training, right on down to the cooks—all Denny's workers had to watch the video. Training management about racial sensitivity also had to be done in live situations, using in-person interactions as well as videotapes. In a later chapter, we'll walk you through a part of the managerial training process.

A Different Kind of Agreement

The consent decree was a legally binding agreement among our company, the U.S. Department of Justice, and counsel for the plaintiff class. But in July 1993, Flagstar, through my predecessor, Jerry Richardson, entered into a morally binding agreement—what's known as a fair share agreement—between the company and the NAACP. This agreement established a set of numerical targets concerning the ways we would expand our business among minority vendors as well as the ways we would expand the presence of minorities within Denny's and all of Flagstar.

This agreement had a history that preceded the consent decree; though we finalized it in 1993, it had its origins in another incident that occurred at one of our Quincy's restaurants. Still, the NAACP, which is the oldest and largest civil rights organization in the United States, had made moves from the start to support the plaintiffs in the Christina Ridgeway complaint. It was clear that the group would seek to expand the scope beyond simply remedying the slights and insults that had befallen individual customers, to ensuring that Flagstar's atonement also became an instrument of black economic expansion. The fair share agreement Flagstar signed was similar to other such agreements the NAACP had negotiated with many other large corporations over the years.

For one reason or another—usually because the companies got into trouble somehow, as Denny's had, or because they already had a large black customer base that gave them a vested interest in working with representatives of the black community—the NAACP has been very successful in getting companies to agree to specific targets to work toward, in areas such as purchasing, franchising, and employment, all things that would serve to aid black economic development. Some businesspeople consider the group's posture as equivalent to extortion, particularly in the effective way the NAACP brings public pressure on corporations to sign these agreements.

I couldn't disagree more. The truth is Denny's was knee-deep in problems in 1993; it needed direction in how to right itself. I don't believe that Denny's could have achieved all that it has—and all that it continues to achieve—without the starting point of the fair share agreement that was signed.

The fair share agreement took the matter of how Denny's treated minorities beyond a civil rights matter and into the sphere of economic development. Prior to this agreement, we had only one black franchise owner, no black person on the board of directors, no black advertising agencies, and very, very few contracts with black-owned professional service providers and vendors. Just as Denny's had distanced itself from minority consumers, alienating millions of potential customers, it had also virtually shut out minority business owners, closing itself off to the possibility of fruitful business partnerships with black entrepreneurs as well as other people of color in business. So the targets in the fair share agreement were developed to remedy this situation. Over a seven-year period, we agreed to do many things that we thought would prove our honorable intentions to the NAACP and aid minority business development.

Like everything concerned with this corporate transformation, some of the aims we agreed on with the NAACP were fairly easy to implement. For instance, the company agreed to put at least one African-American director on its board of directors. We did that almost immediately, with the selection of Dr. Vera King Farris, president of the Richard Stockton College of New Jersey, in December 1993.

Denny's also agreed to boost the number of minority franchises to at least 54. We also said we would attempt to have the number of minority managers at Denny's mirror the ratio of minorities in the population as a whole. That meant we were promising at least 12% of our managers would be minorities. Under the terms of the fair share agreement, we established these goals for the end of 1996, and agreed to review them in 1997 to set new goals that would take us through 2000, which we did.

As far as our advertising and marketing commitment was concerned, we said that by the end of the seven-year period of the agreement, we would be investing at least 10% of our marketing and advertising budget with minority-owned ad agencies. To help us reach African-American and Hispanic customers more effectively, we now work with minority-owned advertising agencies. The Chisholm-Mingo Group, Inc. in New York specializes in marketing to African-Americans, and in Dallas, Siboney USA targets Hispanic customers. With the assistance of these agencies, we spend more than $13 million annually to reach important minority market segments.

Clearly, a large amount of the money we spend each year is on food and other supplies for our restaurants. But virtually none of the businesses that supplied those goods in the early 1990s were minority-owned firms. So another part of the fair share agreement was to meet a goal of having minority vendors account for at least 12% annually of paper, food, and other supplies. And there were goals for other professional services, too, in addition to marketing and advertising and promotion—things like legal services. Denny's agreed that at the end of seven years, expenditures on these services would amount to a minimum of 13% of the total the company spent on services in that category.

In some ways, 1993 was Flagstar's toughest year; it looked to outsiders—even me—as though the company was about to fall apart. Public humiliation, painful revelations, and a vague sense of shame took its toll on many good people who worked for this company. But even amid what looked like destruction, there were men and women at Flagstar who had begun the struggle to rebuild our business and our honor. Sure, we had legal obligations to improve the way we did business, but those obligations were only a minimum standard. Sure, it was a good public relations move to enter into an agreement with the NAACP, but their goals became our starting points. To change our culture, to change our reputation, it would take a lot more than the minimum. I was prepared to take these basic tools left by my predecessors and, along with a first-rate and committed team, build the best and fairest workplace in America.

Leading the Way

The work we needed to accomplish at Denny's was an enormous task—there was no way I could do it all myself. Every person in every department needed to get on board and become committed to the sense that we were the best restaurant chain in America. I couldn't make them do anything, but I could set an example. I could lead the way as Denny's reinvented itself. I could be clear about what my commitment was. I could be clear about what to expect. I could be clear about the consequences if people didn't share my commitment to good food, reasonable prices, great service, and a respectful atmosphere.

All those things, and others, come from the top. When other executives ask me what we did to turn this company around—and I get asked this a lot—the first thing I tell them is that this is a mission that gets accomplished from the highest levels of the organization to the lowest.

Somebody has to lead. As chairman and CEO, that some-one is me.

Another crucial part of effective leadership involves hir-ing the people who can help you meet your goals. You need to find the people with the same capacity for passion about the work, who understand what you want for the company and are on fire to make it happen. You have to treat those people, once you find them, with respect and appreciation. You have to be capable of listening to and learning some-thing new from the people who work for you. Diversity is not just about race and gender; it's also about opinions and perspectives on a situation. To lead, you need the flexibility and the self-confidence to admit that you don't know every-thing. When you're paying people for their talents and expertise, they need to be free to use all their skills, as well as their love and enthusiasm for the work, to do their very best. It matters very much how we treat one another, in the workplace and outside it. As a leader, I want to model that for all the people of this company; I want to walk that talk.

The good we have accomplished at Denny's and through-out the other divisions of Advantica could never have been brought about by a single person. But if there is one person who has led the way in moving us toward an inclusive work-place, it would have to be Ray Hood-Phillips, our chief diversity officer. Without her spirit and her vision, her enthusiasm and her faith in our capacity for change, we never could have come as far as we have.

Tearing Down Barriers

I first met Ray several years ago when she was working at Burger King, where she eventually became vice president of human resources. Ray grew up in central-city Detroit and graduated from Michigan State University, where she eventually earned her master of arts degree in communication arts and science. Ray also had a long track record in advertising and marketing at major agencies in the Midwest. Just as important, though, are the experience and understanding she brings from her personal life as an African-American woman. She often tells audiences, "I've experienced it—the inequities, the glass ceiling, and all that stuff." "I could tell stories that would make my colleagues' hair stand on end. But all the things that have happened to me helped me understand more about what I'm doing now, about how you begin to tear down the barriers between people."

Ray began tearing down those barriers when she arrived at Burger King in 1984; upon her arrival there, she was the highest-ranking black woman in the company. She worked for two years in advertising and marketing before she was asked to start a new department—that of minority affairs. To some degree, that new department was a response to earlier charges of discrimination and lack of opportunity made by minority franchisees and suppliers against Burger King in 1982 and 1983. As a result, Operation PUSH had threatened a boycott of the company. It was the specter of that boycott that led the company to ask Ray to take charge of this volatile issue. She remembers that when they asked her to lead this new department, her boss promised her she'd have to spend only two years on it. They wanted her to help them set up the office and show them what they ought to do, and then she could go back to her job in marketing. She absolutely didn't want to do it at first, but Ray's a very devout woman with a strong faith. And when she took the weekend to think about it and pray over it, she finally agreed.

By the time I arrived at Burger King, Ray had created an incredible program. She'd brought in consultants, and together they had designed a very tough yet compassionate and focused diversity training program that got people really talking about what they were feeling around issues of racial and ethnic diversity. Participants had to sign statements of confidentiality, promising that what was said in the group would remain privileged information. In this way, group members eventually could feel safe enough to share their fears and prejudices about different groups of people. The purpose was not just to get them to vent. The idea was to address systemic issues, to give workers a chance both to expose their feelings and, in Ray's words, "to show people how to build productive, collaborative partnerships across lines of difference."

It was a tough time at Burger King at that point; there had been a fair amount of downsizing and people were concerned about job security. Whenever folks feel threatened, of course, there's a lot of distrust. But Ray had put together these three-day sessions with 20 to 25 people, and Barry Gibbons was so impressed by the training she and her people designed that he wanted all the executives to go through the training immediately. That was my first experience with diversity training similar to the kind of training we do here at Advantica.

So not long after I arrived here, when I could tell I had a bigger problem than I'd first imagined, the first person I thought of was Ray. At that time, she had started her own consulting business and was doing work for Burger King. I called her and said, "I need some big-time help here." Part of me hesitated about calling her, even though she was the very best person for this disaster we were facing at Denny's. For years, while we'd worked at Burger King, I'd been telling Ray, "There is more that you can do. You can help run a business. You could head the marketing department of a very big business." But I also knew that doing this work on diversity and inclusion was her passion and her life.

Because she wanted to help me, she agreed that she'd consult for two or three days a week. So Ray would get up at three o'clock in the morning to take a dawn flight from Miami to Spartanburg. By 9:30 A.M., she'd be in our offices. The original plan was that she'd look through everything, examine the consent decree, then recommend what we ought to do, the kind of people we should hire, and what programs we ought to implement to start turning the company around.

It didn't take long for Ray to become engrossed in the work. She said to me at one point, "This is huge! The opportunity is so large, and there's nowhere to go but up, given our public image and everything that's happened." After a few months of working 18-hour days, Ray decided to cast her lot with us and move to Spartanburg. She joined us in April 1995.

Ray likes to remind me of a time when we were having a dialogue with a group of executives about our outlook on diversity and inclusiveness. At one point, in speaking to that group, I said, "You know, we need to be color-blind; we can't see color." Ray told me later that she knew she would have to approach me about that, but she wanted to wait until we were alone.

Once we were out the door, she pulled me aside and said, "I need to talk with you a second." Well, she really took me out to the woodshed that day. Ray was very up front about disagreeing with me about so-called color blindness. All human beings have differences, she said; people of different racial and ethnic backgrounds have different cultural and social references and thus couldn't think or act in the same ways. "Jim, we do have differences; you need to recognize that," she said to me. Thank goodness I had the sense to listen to her. A lot of the progress we've made in becoming a diverse and inclusive company occurred because we stopped pretending that everyone in the United States is the same. They aren't, and they don't have to be. But we are all equal; we all have the same rights and privileges. It sounds like a small distinction, but for us, it was a distinction that made all the difference.

"When I came to the company, I found really enthusiastic people who needed direction in this very specific area," she said. "A lot of good things were already in place. People were working diligently. They wanted to get it right. We just needed to put it into a strategy."

That's been Ray's focus since her arrival—helping our people get it right. Ray has been our point person in this quest. She worked with our training department, for example, to oversee the diversity training sessions at every level of our company, training that is mandatory for every worker at Denny's. She works with Karen Regan (whom you'll hear more about later), who built from the ground up the materials and the structure that equip all our people to work with an incredibly varied population.

Along with changes like this, Ray helped us develop initiatives to monitor progress in every area of our operations—our purchasing contracts, management positions, training and education, marketing, philanthropic contributions, franchising, performance evaluations, even our reciprocal trade partnerships with minority groups. In addition, she pays close attention to the strategic decisions and actions of our senior management committee as well as of our board of directors.

What made her work so vital to our success was that before she came, we had no consistent way of tracking our workforce. Once she and her team had a system in place, we could keep track of our workforce, know whether we were making progress, and immediately see areas for improvement. About two years into this process, I was able to add some incentives to my efforts to change the company culture. Because I could effectively monitor the progress of senior management, I could begin to tie 25% of the senior management team's incentive bonus to the advancement of women and people of color. That wouldn't have been possible without Ray's hard work, her organizational skills, and her powers of persuasion.

The president of our Denny's unit, John Romandetti, has often commented about the phenomenal spirit and enthusiasm that she brings to her work. "I get tired just looking at Ray, she has so much energy. I've known her for a lot of years. ... Her optimism is just amazing. I love it; I love glass-half-full kind of people. Ray is not only 'half-full'—she really overflows."

Though she sits on the management committee, "I have very little direct control," she said recently. "It is ninety percent influence and trying to help people understand this is good for us—for the team and for business."

The truth is that Ray Hood-Phillips and her leadership have been good for us, and her presence has been a gift to our company. She's a woman of great heart and great integrity; I seek her counsel on every major problem we have.

Hands-On Leadership

I was blessed, at the start of my tenure here, to have Ron Petty as the head of the Denny's unit. He'd preceded me at Flagstar and was hired from Miami Subs in the wake of Denny's lawsuits and the consent decrees. From the very start, Ron was committed to putting behind us the ugliness of the previous two years. Several people have commented on the core of people who have joined me here from Burger King Corporation. But the truth is that Ron Petty got here first! My predecessor hired him in July 1993, one of Richardson's first responses to the claims of discrimination. It was Ron who took a key role in the company's initial efforts to alter the corporate culture. The examination of day-to-day procedures and policies, the initial efforts to review and revise our systems and to fight the perception of racism with the reality of great service—these tasks initially fell to Ron.

He joined Denny's at what was probably the worst point in its history. It was Ron's vision, determination, and sense of immediacy that helped to reverse the company's downward slide in the eyes of the public. Though he arrived in July, by the end of 1993 Denny's had received more than 600 inquiries from people of color concerning the possibility of franchise ownership. More than 100 applications were sent out and by year's end, about 55 applications were in their final stages of review; the number of black managers increased from 4.4% to 6.7% in Ron's first six months on the job—pretty quick work.

Ron also knew that in addition to the internal work of change, how our restaurants looked mattered as well; what quicker way to broadcast our intention to make a brand-new Denny's? It was Ron who started the systemwide renovations of our restaurants, including changes in menus, new cooking equipment, and more contemporary uniforms. Not long after I arrived, a large portion of Denny's repositioning had already been accomplished. When Ron got an opportunity to fulfill his lifelong dream of heading up an entrepreneurial effort, I reluctantly said good-bye, with full support for his new endeavor and with a lot of gratitude for the groundwork he'd laid.

Once I knew I had to replace Ron, I didn't have to look any farther than one of our other units—El Pollo Loco, a 250-plus-unit restaurant chain based in Irvine, California. John Romandetti had joined El Pollo Loco in December 1995 after spending 14 years at—you guessed it—Burger King, where he was vice president of operations for the western region of the United States.

John told me that when I called to ask whether he was interested in heading up the Denny's unit, he had to take a deep breath and think about it for a few days. I didn't try to sell John on the job, but I did want him to know the full facts. As I suspected, though, John was eager to work in what was clearly a turnaround situation. He could sense the challenge of it; that was what intrigued him most. In addition, he admitted that it was, as he said, "a pretty cool opportunity" to move from running a regional brand like El Pollo Loco to a national brand like Denny's. No, he wasn't wild about the stigma associated with Denny's. But like the rest of us, he believed there was nowhere to go but up. He was prepared for the looks of pity and surprise that wounded so many of our employees when telling others where they worked. But John also had confidence that as we continued to make changes, we would also be able to make our case to Americans.

John was asked once about his experience in Burger King with the Diversity Action Council (DAC), of which Ray Hood-Phillips also was a part. His comments were very interesting and, to a great degree, mirror my own. He was an active participant in DAC and enjoyed the work. But he often says that for him, what you need most in the end is common sense and a respect for human dignity. If you're brought up right, John says, you understand how to deal with people—you understand what's right and what's wrong. You understand how to hold people accountable, and then you just go do it. And you make sure that everybody around you does the same thing.

I liked John for the job because of his ethics, his skills in operations, and his powerful strategic insight. He's a very detail-oriented man, and I knew no aspect of Denny's would go untouched. I was sure he would make an immediate difference. John likes to say that his big leadership task was to remedy what he called a deficiency of knowledge on many levels of the company. He's worked with so many wonderful and committed people here at our company who nonetheless had few ways to understand and learn more about how we can best do our jobs. A big part of leadership involves hiring the best people, giving them the tools they need to work, and trusting them to get the job done.

Some of the policies and procedures instituted by Ron and his team were working; some weren't. It was a fairly common scenario at a time of great change in corporate culture. So when John arrived, two or three years after the heat of initial change, he had the benefit of being able to review what had been done before deciding what was left to do and how we might all get there. John thinks that what he was able to bring to the company was more discipline in the processes and procedures we used. John was able to infuse the system with a lot more follow-up, to communicate a much greater sense of urgency to those who thought that they could treat somebody differently and get away with it. He and his team made it abundantly clear that for people who hadn't yet gotten our message, their employment with our company would be brief.

It was that sense of urgency that we all brought to the process, led by John Romandetti, which sent such a strong message to the system as a whole. His leadership helped to make it clear that on the issue of creating a diverse and inclusive company, we were taking no prisoners. We took it seriously then; we take it seriously now.

As I said, leadership means getting the best people you can to do a job, then letting them do it. That's why I got John to come to Flagstar in the first place. We had known each other for several years, of course, and that helps. He knew what kind of person I was, and I knew what kind of person he was. Certainly what John knew and appreciated about me was my style of hiring good people and then leaving them alone, not micromanaging their every move. Now, some people confuse that with a lack of accountability, and they're wrong. As a leader, you've got to know what people are doing in their areas of responsibility and why they've made the choices they have. If something isn't working, you've got to get straight answers, and sometimes, when folks aren't working out, you have to let them go. But just as important, I think, is the quality of trust. You've got to trust in your own judgment in hiring the men and women whom you think are the best. You've got to trust in those people to do their best for you and for the company. John and I would discuss issues as often as he needed. John is an independent operator, however, and I trusted him. That made for an excellent fit.

I'm especially sensitive to the possible confusion that can result when people think of me as the face of change at Denny's. It's true, I'm ultimately responsible for what happens here. But it is John who bears the day-to-day responsibility for our work and our success in turning the company around, just as Ron Petty bore the responsibility before him. Leadership also, to my mind as well as John's, means putting the good of the company first, ahead of the visibility that might accrue to one or the other of us. We both have the same end result in mind: a profitable company we can be proud of. Each of us has many opportunities to get across the message that Denny's is a different place than it used to be. And so we coexist pretty well. There are moments when it can present complex issues, particularly from the restaurants' perspective. John has to manage that issue because he runs the brand, not me. There are moments when there could be confusion on such points because I don't do my people's work for them. But John has shown himself more than capable of working through issues like this.

The Face of Change

Being willing to lead—being able to lead—means being able to stand your ground in spite of public opinion. I've had a lot of practice in that area since I arrived at Denny's; so have most of my key people. When your company is the subject of scorn all over the country, when comedians on national television make you their targets, when even family members ask you what on earth you're doing working for "a company like that," leadership means being clear with yourself what it is that you're doing and why it is that you're doing it. It's also about taking that message to the people with whom you work, making certain they feel sure of your resolve to fix the problem, challenging every false report with the truth of what you're doing, and most of all, making sure that you're correcting the problems rather than denying them or running away.

John does a good job of that, wherever he goes. Once he was asked whether it was difficult to tell people that he was the CEO of Denny's. He said that after people gave him a look of horror or made some pointed comment about how many lawsuits he'd handled that week, he took the opportunity whenever he could to chat with that person about what it is we're really doing here. John's found—and it's been true for many of us—that people are completely blown away by the statistics we can give about what kind of changes we've made here. They want to talk about how it is that nearly half of everyone who works for Denny's are people of color, about how it is that nearly 40% of our franchise owners are people of color.

John has become accustomed to the belief of many people that all our hard work was done because of the "force" inherent in the consent decree. But as John would be the first to tell you—and he's speaking for many of us—the consent decree is in many ways irrelevant to the way we do business. Yes, it exists legally, and we hope that we've proven our commitment to inclusivity enough so that even the need for that decree will soon be a thing of the past. But what's most important to John, to me, to all of us here, is that we would not do anything differently in our management styles without the decree. The facts are plain: The United States is not all white and never was; as businesspeople, we understand that there's a lot of money out there, that if we're responsive and respectful and address people's real needs, we've got a much better shot at getting a larger share of those dollars.

As business leaders, we can't and shouldn't be embarrassed by wanting to make money—that's a big part of our jobs. But that's not the only thing we do. We have made the commitment to hire America. It's not something that you ever stop thinking about, because once you do, that is precisely when you start seeing the numbers contract. John and I know the importance of the bottom line. But I think it is equally important for business leaders to recognize the increasing diversity in the country and the benefits of having an increasingly diverse senior management team (which I believe we have). By doing so, I believe you inculcate that operating philosophy by example. Leadership means walking the talk so that the company culture can see what you do and can follow it.

Leadership can also mean being out front, an easy target for the contempt of an angry nation. That's the position that Karen Randall found herself in when I arrived. Now the vice president of communications for Advantica, she has worked in the field of public relations for more than 20 years, a good portion of that time for our company. More directly than anyone, Karen Randall has spent years facing down all the perceptions and charges of racism that Denny's has had to endure. Her years of experience in weathering this crisis taught her some valuable lessons about the importance of diversity and its relationship to public relations as well as public opinion. As she wrote in her case study of the company for her master's thesis:

> The biggest mistake [we] made was that [our] company was several years behind in diversity. Since the company had virtually no track record with African-Americans ... the company was vulnerable. ... Without a track record in diversity, there was no quick fix for Denny's problems.

Karen concluded in another article that "conventional public relations wisdom is to get your side of the story out fast. Usually, that is not enough. It is important for a company to look internally and determine whether change is needed." In Karen's case, leadership means standing with your company against an onslaught of negative publicity in virtually every medium and attempting to tell the stories of the small successes until the larger successes can be gained. Leadership also means going back to the media that savaged your company and encouraging them to tell the rest of the story—something Karen has done with great success. From the scornful and negative articles and columns of 1994, we can point to the upbeat stories of our turnaround, in every venue from *Fortune* magazine to *USA Today* to *60 Minutes*. Throughout it all, Karen has managed to keep her composure, even when the coverage of our predicament has been at its most negative, leading the rest of us through the process of sharing with the world the good news about Denny's and all of Advantica.

There are so many ways to lead, and I feel grateful that I have so many people working here with the capacity to do just that. Let's say, for example, that I leave in another year or so, or John leaves in a year or so. What happens to Denny's? I say Denny's gets better and better. Why? Because there's enough commitment here to change. There are enough individuals in this company today who are forever changed, as a result of our work together—John Romandetti, Ray Hood-Phillips, Rob Barrett, Karen Randall, and so many others—that this company would never again be the way it used to be.

Training Our Employees to Be the Best

I love listening to Joel Gonzalez. He's a young man who started working for Denny's in 1980 as a service assistant in Oklahoma City. Back then, of course, nobody called people in his position service assistants—Joel was a busboy. He's still with us. Joel doesn't carry dishes to the kitchen anymore, though. Now he trains many of our managers, servers, and other restaurant personnel in the many ways we can make Denny's a better place for our customers. Find Joel—as you might have in 1998, in a nondescript Houston hotel meeting room—and you'll see what I mean.

In the workshop he was conducting then, Joel threw off a focused energy that filled the room, drawing in participants and holding their attention for hours. There were about a dozen people in attendance during that session, drawn from Denny's restaurants all over the region. These managers were men and women of Asian-American,

Hispanic, African-American, and white European descent. The gathering was as diverse a group as you can imagine, a group that reflects not only the new face of Denny's but, increasingly, the new face of the country.

Up front, Joel and his cotrainer, Ron Narum (a former restaurant manager and longtime employee now working in our human resources department) were putting the participants through their paces, repeating the mantra of the morning. "Perception is reality," Ron told the group. "Perception is reality," he said again. Those words are one key to the way we train our managers. We don't mean to suggest that a customer who has felt discriminated against is making it all up. We know there have been incidents of actual discrimination at our restaurants. It is, in fact, why our discrimination policy is clearly stated to the managers attending this session and to all our employees:

> Denny's is committed to maintaining a harassment- and discrimination-free environment for all guests and employees. We are committed to treating all guests and fellow employees with dignity and respect. We do not discriminate against any guest or employee on the basis of race, color, religion, national origin, disability, sex, sexual orientation, or age.

We also know, however, that our employees have to be aware of the way customers feel when they eat at Denny's; that knowledge is important, too. These managers didn't leave this training without understanding that.

The group was good-natured, laughing as they started this day-long workshop, one of our basic training methods. They came dressed casually; soft-soled shoes, casual pants and no ties for the men; loose-fitting blouses and skirts, or pants for the women. Despite the casual dress and the easygoing atmosphere, serious work was going on. These men and women were to participate in training exercises, experience some surprises, perhaps even discover some things about themselves. In the end, if the men and women in this room remembered only two things that cut to the heart of our work in this area, those things would be first, our no-nonsense nondiscrimination policy, and second, the words of the day—"Perception is reality."

Knowing intimately the full meaning of that phrase and thoroughly understanding our company's nondiscrimination policy are the fundamental goals of our training work. By the time our people have finished their mandated training courses—all managers must take two one-day training sessions—they know that they cannot discriminate against any of our customers. They also know that when it comes to dealing with displeased customers, often what the customer *thinks* happened counts as much as what really did happen. These managers will learn ways to put themselves in the customers' place—something Ron and Joel insisted on during the various role-playing exercises.

Managers in these workshops discover, though, that they can put themselves in the customers' place only up to a certain point. During training, Joel told one manager about handling an irate customer: "Don't say, 'I know how you feel.' He'll easily say back to you, 'How do you know how I feel? You're not black like me. Where are you coming from with that?'" So employees are taught not just *to* empathize with the customer but also *how* to empathize with the customer and to reflect back to that customer concern about the problem. It's not always an easy thing to do. As Ron told the group, "We'll never completely understand what goes on in somebody else's life. That's why we stay away from saying things like 'I know how you feel.'" It is this mix of practical and theoretical training that helps make clear to our managers what they have to do at Denny's.

You could say that much of what these people are learning is a new twist on an old saying that businesspeople have placed their faith in for years: "The customer is always right." Well, the customer isn't always right, of course. But if you don't treat customers as if they are, then they will be right about one thing: You aren't listening and you're being disrespectful. Our employees owe it to customers to correct the problem to the best of their abilities, before it becomes more serious. This is what all our employees know now. They may just chalk up the fact that the meal didn't come on time to a slow server and a stressed-out cook. But when that meal fails to materialize for a black customer, and the server doesn't bother to explain why, and no one can find the manager because he or she is standing in for a cook who is out sick ... well, you get the idea.

At one point during the training workshop, the managers looked at a brief video clip about managing escalation—how to effectively communicate with a guest who is upset. We've created these tapes with actors in simulated situations, and they are great training tools for us. In this particular clip, a black customer is kept waiting for at least 15 minutes for his order to be taken, whereas white customers are immediately seated and served. When the irate customer asks the server for an explanation, the hapless server turns to him and replies, "They tip."

The lesson to be learned in all of this was how the restaurant personnel could defuse a potentially explosive situation. In addition to approaching the customer with genuine sincerity, there are very specific techniques for defusing the situation—getting to eye level with the customer, really listening to what is being said, acknowledging that what happened was wrong, and reflecting back to the customer what he or she has said. And, of course, there should be a sincere apology. All these are among the techniques a manager can use to talk with an upset customer. Strangely, however, there was one silver lining in the dark cloud of racism raised by this incident after the managers saw it. Later, when Ron and Joel had separated the larger group into pairs who role-played the aftermath of the situation, a woman who was one of the participants in the workshop looked toward Joel and asked, mouth agape, "This really happened?"

Not by Accident

It's wonderful that some people who work for us can't imagine that any server at Denny's would ever have treated a customer that way. With 70,000 employees, including the 450 or so who work in Spartanburg, and about 30,000 who work in franchise operations, the overwhelming majority of our employees, I can assure you, are neither thoughtless, incompetent, nor racist. But food service has historically been a "paying your dues" industry, where salaries can be relatively low and the work relatively hard. Outsiders may see everything from independence to glamour to creativity in owning a restaurant. None of that is impossible. But our employees also work hard and long hours, carrying trays, cleaning out bathrooms, emptying grease pans, and standing over the proverbial hot stove. This behind the scenes work is continuous because most Denny's are open around the clock. That's why we spend as much time and energy as we do on training the really good people we find.

We do have to show specific tapes and use specific workshop materials under the consent decree. Although I used to be ambivalent about how useful training ultimately is, I've concluded that it is an invaluable tool. Not only do these programs make very clear what is expected of our employees but they also give our employees the tools to meet those obligations and responsibilities. Although we tell our people how to handle bad situations in the restaurant and how to work with them when they do happen, no training is successful without accountability. That means that Denny's employees know from the start that they face penalties for not living up to what we expect of them. This can mean anything from having their actions noted in their personnel files to outright termination, but I like to think of all of our training tools as providing guidance rather than threatening sanctions.

We have gotten tremendous results from the training methods we have used. How good are the results? So strong that we were released from the oversight of the Office of the Civil Rights Monitor (OCRM) December 31, 1999, more than one year ahead of schedule. Just because we are no longer facing daily oversight by a court-appointed civil rights monitor, however, that doesn't mean that Denny's will stop its efforts to become a diverse, inclusive, and nondiscriminatory company. We're obviously staying the course. Our training functions were put completely under our control in April 1999, and now we conduct our own investigations of any complaints of discrimination. All in all, I'd say that's a pretty good way to usher in the new millennium.

As chairman and CEO, I don't oversee the training activities. We need the right people to do that. Fortunately, I didn't have to go any farther than our own system to find the right one. To make sure our training activities run smoothly, I rely heavily on people like Karen Regan, Advantica's director of diversity training, and the talented team she has assembled. Karen's an old hand, with a good sense of the history of our company, both the good parts and the not so good. She's been here since the early 1980s, starting with our Quincy's Family Steakhouse units. We no longer have the Quincy's chain, which was located mainly in the southeastern United States; it was sold during our restructuring. But we've hung on to Karen. She has spent more than 15 years in the training department, taking advantage of our company's long-standing tradition of rewarding good work from the inside.

Even before the incidents in San Jose and Annapolis forced Denny's to be sensitive to all its customers, the chain was working on the sort of initiatives that would stand it in good stead with its guests. It's a bit ironic to go back to our annual report from 1991, when we were TW Holdings, Inc., and read lines like the following:

> Denny's is adapting to changing customer preferences for service. Our service personnel are trained to provide the kind of service customers want. ... Since 1989 Denny's has become well known for its Ten-Minute Service Guarantee...

That guarantee, which promised that breakfast and lunch orders would be served within 10 minutes, has been discontinued. It just wasn't practical. In the early 1990s, Karen and the rest of the team were really focusing on how to make the company the best food service company in the world by the turn of the twenty-first century. The vehicle for doing that was a master plan for the entire company as it existed back then, when the main restaurant units were Denny's, Hardee's, Quincy's, and El Pollo Loco. Called Mission 2000, the program began in the early 1990s, prior to my arrival. To implement Mission 2000, TW Services, as the company was called then, hired the first of many consultants that it would bring in over the next half dozen years.

The group that helped the company develop a mission statement that would encompass every part of its operations was Synectics, a consulting firm in Cambridge, Massachusetts. Synectics wasn't brought in specifically to train people in attitudes on race and how those attitudes can manifest themselves on the job. It was only two years after TW consolidated its various operations in Spartanburg in 1989. So the Mission 2000 program concentrated on the broadest possible goal. It was a catalyst for changes that we planned to mold TW into the top food service company in the world.

The good intentions of the Mission 2000 program were lost in the subsequent financial reorganizations. With the company struggling just to stay out of bankruptcy, the initiatives developed under Mission 2000, such as getting the food to the customer in 10 minutes or developing take-out orders, couldn't be maintained, let alone expanded upon. Add to that the subsequent changes in management and ownership, as well as the impact of the court cases, and it's easy to see why the focus on Mission 2000 fell by the wayside.

So why talk about it at all? I bring it up to correct a common misperception about Denny's: the idea that no one here had ever given any thought to the idea of train-ing our restaurant managers in the importance of the diversity of our customers until the company was forced by consent decree to confront the issue head-on. Mission 2000 established the groundwork for some of the more successful training programs we have developed since the early 1990s.

Karen Regan, for instance, looks back on at least one Mission 2000 project, the "listening sessions." They're what some people call focus groups, and they were held with employees across the country in 1990. Says Karen, "These were among the company's first attempts to understand how our employees felt about the company and what would make it great. It wasn't anything that was handed down from above, either. It was the requests and comments of hourly employees." Among the issues discussed was diver-sity; in fact, the employees demanded that this issue be somehow addressed. Many of those employees were minori-ties. When they repeatedly asked their managers to consider how they felt about them as well as about customers who looked like them, it was hard not to hear. But it was too easy, I'm afraid, not to listen.

Still, there was some action from those groups. But it did-n't come until after the negative press started to hit the com-pany in the wake of the Ridgeway and other California cases. In July 1992, the company developed its first diversity committee. This was the committee that recommended to my predecessor, Jerry Richardson, that Flagstar enter into negotiations with the NAACP. The diversity committee comprised of people from every level of the organization, from hourly workers to senior-level managers. It was also ethnically diverse and included African-Americans, women, white men, Latinos, and Asian-Americans. Altogether there were about a dozen members, although sometimes as many as 18 sat in on meetings.

The diversity committee was organized informally, though it was hard working, to be sure. One of the first things that this group did, working in cramped rooms in Spartanburg for three days running, was to try to figure out how to make diversity something real for our employees and managers.

One consultant was particularly helpful on the diversity front, even that far back in Denny's and Advantica's history. That was IEC Enterprises, a diversity consulting firm based in Atlanta, Georgia. Karen attended one of their programs in Atlanta so that she "could come back and share with the rest of that committee what a diversity initiative looked like," she says. Discussions between Karen and IEC and later among members of that internal committee during late 1992 and early 1993 slowly started to bear fruit. They looked at other companies that were models for managing diversity back then to see what they could learn. Sara Lee Corp., for example, especially at its plant in nearby Winston-Salem, North Carolina, was regularly recognized as being a success in terms of the diversity of its workforce.

Much of the energy in this area at the time stemmed from what other companies were doing and how they were working with their managers to respect, value, and profit from a diverse world. The whole diversity movement, in fact, was only about 10 years old in 1992. Although corporations had become relatively accustomed to affirmative action and what that meant, many of my peers in the corporate world did not understand that affirmative action, no matter how earnest, wasn't going to meet all the needs of the corporation and of the marketplace as each became more diverse.

One of the seminal thinkers and writers in this area is Roosevelt Thomas. I know Karen, our current director of diversity training, has read his work. His book, *Beyond Race and Gender: Unleashing the Power of Your Total Work Force by Managing Diversity*, was one of the earliest books on diversity, and one that has heavily influenced the corporate thinking here about training for diversity. His latest book, *Building a House for Diversity: How a Fable about a Giraffe and Elephant Offers New Strategies for Today's Workforce*, also addresses some of the questions that have proved important to us in these issues. I recommend them both highly. You can certainly see the basics of Thomas's ideas here now, when he writes about what he calls "diversity mature" corporations and what they need:

> ...a comprehensive mission and vision, and a diversity management mission and vision. The first serves as the glue that holds different and disparate people and organizations together. The second provides motivation for corporatewide efforts to build diversity effectiveness.

By 1992 and early 1993, this company hadn't quite managed to merge those two missions. It was either trying to revamp the whole corporation, as with the Mission 2000 program, or developing diversity training programs without really linking them to the company's most pressing corporate concerns. In the wake of the Ridgeway incident in San Jose, Flagstar instituted some localized employee training to teach workers how to be more sensitive to a diverse customer base. The management training workshops, which took place in April and May 1992, were prepared for Denny's by another consulting firm in California. The idea was to train managers in the San Jose market in a way that would help them avoid incidents that stemmed from discriminatory actions. Like the eventual We Can series, the basic training tool we use now (which Joel and Ron teach), it was a two-day workshop with role-playing and exercises. But it fell short. Although the workshop explored and helped explain the pitfalls of not being sensitive to differences of ethnicity, it didn't link that knowledge to working in restaurants. Says Karen Regan, who observed some of these sessions, "They helped people understand their own feelings around these issues, but they didn't necessarily tell people how to handle them. The problem was that it left people feeling guilty. You might walk away disturbed by some of the things you learned about your own beliefs and might not know what to do with those feelings. I think that's one reason diversity training might be a bitter pill for some people." In one exercise, participants would be placed in a mock meeting where they were asked to treat one another according to some stereotype set earlier, and secretly, by the rest of the group. The person selected would invariably end up behaving according to the stereotype that the others expected him to demonstrate. It was the self-fulfilling prophecy; treat people as if they'll behave badly and some of them will, making your prediction true. Evidently that lesson took some people at Denny's back then by surprise. Those workshops might even have led to some individual soul-searching. Aside from how it left the participants feeling, however, there was another problem with these training sessions: they were not specifically focused on the restaurant business.

There were other false starts at training our staff. The company hired a noted California consultant, a woman who had been actively participating in many of the efforts to rebuild Los Angeles following the devastating riots there in 1992. Karen and the folks from Denny's met with her and her staff in the spring of 1993 and explained that Denny's was looking to sensitize its restaurant managers to diversity issues at a series of workshops across the country. So far, so good. Says Karen, "At one workshop, one of their facilitators opened the training session by saying something like 'If I were not teaching people at this company, I'd be suing Denny's, too!'" When word of that spread throughout the company, people were furious. Another disagreement arose when the consulting firm insisted that every workshop participant make a list of his or her prejudices, sign it, and hand it in to the facilitators. That was certainly an idea that did not go over well at all. Denny's quickly regrouped and brought in IEC Enterprises to complete the workshops.

We learned from our past experiences, though. In a process of continual improvement, we ultimately learned some important things about what makes training effective. One is that we have to develop the training programs ourselves to ensure that they are relevant to our business. The diversity training programs were mandated by the consent decrees, but we had discovered along the way that using outside consultants to actually conduct the training sessions was counterproductive. Employees did not view them as credible. So we decided to develop our own programs and train our own trainers. We sought out the PACE Group, a training consulting firm in Atlanta, to help us come up with a basic framework for designing a training tool that was acceptable to all the parties to the consent decree. We worked with them for two years to produce the We Can workshops.

Trainers? We Grow Our Own

Those workshops, at which we've already gotten a peek, need leaders, a constant stream of Rons and Joels. To get them trained as well as we can, we work with a wonderful organization based in Washington, D.C., the National Coalition Building Institute (NCBI). Their workshops were initially held for about 150 Denny's trainees. Today we send two or three new trainers at a time to NCBI.

The NCBI, in case you are unfamiliar with it, is an organization that was founded in 1984. It is a worldwide organization with the mission of teaching people how to go back to their home communities and, as its name suggests, build the coalitions that will end bigotry and prejudice. In 1995, people from Denny's began going to some of the workshops at NCBI before coming back to our company to help lead the We Can workshops. They go there and are surrounded by a rainbow of people from other business, religious, and education institutions to share in the work of reducing prejudice.

"Denny's has its own model," says NCBI executive director Cherie Brown, referring to our diversity training programs. "But they find our training useful. One of the things that we do here over the three days are what we call speakouts. Those are stories of your life. Participants share stories, good and bad, about the things that have happened to them because of their race, ethnicity, or religion. You don't change their minds; you change their hearts through stories. And I think that it has been very powerful. Many of the

Denny's people who have come have found this very powerful." When our trainers attend a three-day NCBI session, they conduct role-playing exercises where they learn how to talk through difficult issues—often with a racial or ethnic theme—with a diverse group of people. They learn how they can avoid the conflict of the matter and start communicating honestly about the substance of a dispute. "We send people to NCBI now to learn more about themselves and to begin to get some self-knowledge of the things that they can use in the workshops at Denny's," says Karen Regan.

It was fortunate that we found NCBI, but it was also totally by accident, too. "We were in the diversity committee in 1994 when we discovered them," says Karen. "None of the people there knew about them. But the mother of one of our lawyers had worked with them and told her son to check it out." After everything Denny's has been through, we do know that trainers are role models and leaders. If we have our own facilitators, whom our employees see every day in the restaurants and whom they know work for us, not an outsider, it makes a difference. Since 1994, about 300 people from Denny's have made the trip to NCBI as the first step in becoming a Denny's diversity trainer. About half of them are still with us. Trainers can be area managers or human resources managers. Some are restaurant managers, either with company-owned restaurants or at franchises. Franchise employees have to take this course, too, even though they are not employees of Advantica.

We Can, our basic training tool, consists of two days of workshops held at various places around the country—usually a hotel meeting room convenient to everybody, meeting for eight to nine hours a day, with a break for lunch.

Every Denny's manager, field leader, and key employee attends this training. The *Can* in *We Can* stands for *Consistently Attend to guest Needs*. Whereas the primary course gives details of what is expected of every Denny's employee, We Can II is aimed more at specific issues—the types of things we saw Ron and Joel dealing with in that hotel meeting room in Houston. It's less theoretical and a bit more practical in terms of helping our restaurant employees figure out exactly "What do I *do* in this situation?"

Our training group has nicknames for these workshops. We Can I is often referred to as the Old Testament and We Can II as the New Testament. Every management employee must undergo We Can I training within 75 days of being hired or promoted into management, even though the consent decree gives them 90 days. We Can II must be attended within 225 days, even though the consent decree allows 270 days. Most of our new managers and certainly our non-restaurant employees attend the workshops a lot sooner than that.

Then there is a different but similar training videotape that we ask all of our hourly workers to see, generally on the first day of their employment. To make sure that people understand it, we have even translated it in other languages, such as Spanish. Like the We Can tapes, it portrays actors simulating both the wrong and right ways that servers and other hourly workers can handle situations that have the potential to become racially inflammatory.

Denny's CEO, John Romandetti, appears on each tape. Sitting behind a desk, he looks toward the camera and seriously tells the viewer that "some employees have potentially discriminated against minority guests, particularly

African-Americans" and also notes that some have discriminated "unintentionally," before going on to say that "The truth is, Denny's won't survive without minority business." He means it, too. And the hourly workers, among them our servers, are instructed about how to handle some of the situations that have prompted the most concern—how to explain to guests the legitimate reasons for a long wait for food or seating, how not to base service on what a customer's tip is expected to be, or how to be sure not to treat a customer like an "untouchable" by failing to put change in the hand instead of on the counter.

Much of this material is covered in more detail in the We Can tapes seen by managers. We began using We Can I in 1995, and through early 1999 we've given about 2,000 of these workshops around the country, with about 18,000 people attending. We Can II has been taught since early 1997. Through the same period of time, about 12,600 people have attended some 700 classes.

Doing It by the Book

In We Can I, our employees learn the basics:

- They start with a description of the consent decrees and the Civil Rights Act of 1964 and are asked to discuss the consent decree requirements with a partner in the class, explaining in basic terms how they apply to the restaurant. For instance, one of the requirements of the consent decree is that servers must not "offer lesser service" to any person because of race, color, or national origin. Participants are encouraged to discuss what "lesser service" actually means.

- They learn that there is also a protocol, agreed to with the Mexican American Legal Defense and Educational Fund, that prohibits such actions as asking for a "green card" before being served or telling a guest something like "Speak English; you're in America now."

- They learn that if there is a diner who believes that he or she has been discriminated against, then the manager of that restaurant is *required* to give the guest the phone number of Advantica Guest Assurance to report the incident. The manager still has to cooperate fully with a subsequent investigation of the incident. That means interviewing employees for details of the incident if it happens during the shift when the manager is on duty. Although Denny's is not operating under the OCRM after 1999, we still investigate fully any complaints of discriminatory practices.

- They learn that not only may they not indulge in any racial or ethnic discrimination of any kind, especially the use of racial slurs, but that neither may their guests, and that if one does so, he or she is to be asked immediately to leave the restaurant.

- They learn, from their workbooks, what has become a central tenet of this entire experience for Denny's— that *perception is reality*. As the *We Can* workbook says: "When a guest complains of racial discrimination, the manager must deal with the reality that the guest feels discriminated against. Regardless of our own interpretation of what happened, we must deal with the guest's perception of the situation. ... Besides helping us to respond effectively to complaints, raising our level of racial sensitivity can help us eliminate complaints of discrimination in our restaurants." The concluding comment on this page of the workbook is: *Reality is reality*. That means that we recognize that sometimes discriminatory practices do occur and that their occurrence cannot be ruled out until a thorough and complete investigation has been undertaken.

- The participants learn that although their workshops will focus on potential problems of discrimination with regard to African-Americans, any person can experience being the subject of a discriminatory complaint. Those complaints can include a customer alleging that he or she is not being treated as well as other customers, that he or she is being ignored by restaurant personnel; or that another guest has been seated or served before him or her, even though the second guest came into the restaurant after the first. Customer complaints also include general rude and unprofessional treatment and refusal by restaurant personnel to touch the customer, especially in the giving of change.

- They are taught the Prevention Model to reduce the possibility that a customer will feel that he or she has been discriminated against. This is CAN—*consistency* and *communicating*, being *attentive*, and meeting the *needs* of the guest. Here participants are reminded of some of the customer service principles that are basic to the restaurant business. All guests should be treated with dignity and respect. Servers and managers should smile, say "thank you," and make eye contact when talking to diners. The restaurant personnel should ask questions to make sure diners are satisfied with everything and should be sure to listen when customers have complaints. And the server or manager should talk to customers about any service problems *before* the customers form a negative impression because of them. If a diner's meal is late because the grill is down, for example, let the customer know that and head off a potential problem.

- They learn the Intervention Model. This is used when something goes wrong in the dining experience. So what does the server or the restaurant manager do? The three A's: *acknowledge, apologize,* and *act.* We even give our servers and managers help in choosing the words to say to a customer so nothing is left to chance. "I'm really sorry. This doesn't make your experience here acceptable." Of course, any slight variation that conveys the same sentiment and is perceived by the customer as genuine is okay. Then, of course, there must be something the restaurant can do. Offer to do it, employees are told, and then make sure you follow through and tell the guest what you have done.

At the training session in Houston where we started to demonstrate the Intervention Model, Joel asks one of the managers there, "What do you do if the person looks up to you and says, 'You know, that lady ought to be fired; that's what you ought to do—fire her!' Well, you can't fire anyone on the spot," he says. "But you can promise that you will look into the situation and take the appropriate action." In the page of the workshop booklet that describes the Intervention Model, there is a small note at the bottom with an asterisk: "A sincere apology is critical to the successful application of this model." Hey, we don't leave anything to chance when we train our people!

- If the Intervention Model is not working and the guest is still upset, then people are taught to use the final step, the Managing Escalation Model. First, just let the guest vent. Don't say anything. Be quiet and let the diner say what he or she feels needs to be said. Check your body language to make sure you are not sitting or standing in any way that might be construed as hostile. Listen to the emotions from the upset diner as well as the words. Some suggested reflective phrases may then be used, words that will let the diner know that his or her feelings have been recognized: "You sound very angry." "You seem frustrated." "You appear upset." Again, using minor variations of these phrases is perfectly fine to prevent the manager or server from appearing flip or condescending. Then it's time to regroup and go back to the Intervention Model once the decibel level and the anger have subsided.

- Remember the four cardinal "do nots." These are not optional. Never use racial slurs with customers. A manager is never to leave the building to follow a guest, even if it is to apologize. This can be dangerous, the customer can misconstrue it, and in extreme instances, it can leave the manager or server out of sight of other employees if any violent activity occurs. Do not touch a guest, since this could be perceived as a threatening move. And never question anyone's immigration status.

Those are the basics of We Can. Managers watch video clips of these situations and later work with their trainers to identify what exactly is going on. "Is that a reflective statement he is using?" "Does that apology sound sincere?" They will also participate in various exercises that give some help in practicing the skills in the Prevention, Intervention, and Managing Escalation Models after looking at the taped scenarios. Finally, there is an incredible amount of recommended reading material that the participants can avail themselves of at a later date, including these: *To Kill a Mockingbird*, by Harper Lee; *Their Eyes Were Watching God*, by Zora Neale Hurston; *Strangers from a Different Shore: A History of Asian Americans*, by Ronald To Takaki; *Beyond Race and Gender*, by R. Roosevelt Thomas; *Diary of a Young Girl*, by Anne Frank; *The Autobiography of Malcolm X*; and *American Mosaic: The Immigrant Experience in the Words of Those Who Lived It*, by Joan Morrison and Charlotte Fox Zabusky.

Can all this training be done in two days, eight hours each? "Oh, it goes longer than that sometimes, depending on the amount of discussion," says Karen.

The second phase of training, We Can II, reinforces the things that were learned in the first workshop, except in much greater detail. Managers get more experience in role-playing the situations that can cause problems. They learn the specifics about protecting their restaurant and other customers from the inevitable small number of disruptive or offensive customers, and they receive direction on handling their own employees who violate any of Denny's rules, especially those with regard to its discrimination policies.

Let me share with you an example from that We Can II workshop in Houston that Ron and Joel were leading.

"So," says Joel to a new manager, "you're speaking with the customer who has been offended. Do you offer him a free cup of coffee or a free meal?"

"Sure, why not?" comes the reply.

"But don't offer it first of all," says Joel. "That might make the customer angrier. 'What! You think my dignity is worth only $2.99 after what you've done?'"

The class gets the point, and another tip on how to effectively handle a situation has been reinforced. Try to satisfy the customer, but think whether what you are doing to satisfy the guest is an affront to his dignity or could be construed that way. Remember: *Perception is reality.*

We will fire employees who cannot conduct themselves appropriately. Although it does not happen a lot, the situation must be handled correctly when it does arise. In We Can II, the manager learns:

1. To hold the employees accountable for unacceptable behavior.

2. That if the server, for instance, has acted inappropriately by ignoring a customer waiting for service, the manager must report the incident and then set up a time to speak privately with the employee to discuss the problem. The manager has to explain the purpose of the meeting and tell the employee why that particular action was unacceptable. The manager will also talk about other ways the employee could have handled the situation before they agree what to do if a similar situation happens again. The incident is also logged in the employee's file and he or she is warned that failure to comply with the actions that have been agreed upon will result in termination.

3. To discuss the incident with other employees or company personnel, if needed.

4. To follow up with the employee within 30 days to see if the agreed-upon plan of action has been carried out and

to ensure that there are no further incidents.

5. To fire the employee if the behavior does not change. In some egregious instances, such as when an employee uses a racial slur, the employee would be fired immediately.

Now sometimes I am asked if it is possible to "flunk" the workshops. It can happen, but it's a pretty rare occurrence. There have been a few people who were openly hostile to the whole affair. In one situation, a participant at a We Can training session got frustrated at something and became increasingly belligerent. This guy even tossed a book on the floor, which disrupted the workshop. He was asked to leave the workshop, which effectively is being told to leave the company. Since attending these workshops is a condition of employment at Denny's, we notified his supervisor. I don't know if this individual felt persecuted somehow or just did not want to partake in learning what we expected of a Denny's employee. For whatever reason, he is now gone.

Security Works for the Manager, Not the Other Way Around

Training is also important for our security guards, because we have had incidents directly involving them, most notably at a Denny's in Syracuse, New York, where a group of Asian-Americans complained that they were hassled by security guards. The guards were moonlighting police officers. An investigation of that incident by local authorities never proved that any racially discriminatory actions were involved, but it did alert us to the fact that training specially geared toward security guards was needed. We developed this tool, a videotape that all Denny's security guards are required to see, in early 1998, and rolled it out that summer.

We use security guards in many of our restaurants during the late-night shift. Many of the security guards are hired through an agency. Sometimes problems arise because security guards are also off-duty police officers and there is a difference between what an off-duty officer can and should do and what a Denny's employee should do. Our guards are taught that the manager of the restaurant is the boss and that they should take their orders from the manager. Security guards should not intrude into any situation until they are asked to do so by the manager. Often, the guard thinks that his or her quick action will solve the problem before it spirals out of control. That may be true, but the guard still needs to check with the restaurant manager first; otherwise, the guard can end up causing more problems than he or she solves.

For instance, in the training tape, a security guard sees a group of customers leaving the restaurant without stopping at the register. The first time the incident is portrayed, a poorly trained guard rushes out into the street after them. The guard starts to physically restrain one of the group. At that point the tape freezes. What would happen next isn't shown. But it's clear that whatever it is, it will be trouble for all concerned. Then, later on, the correct response is portrayed. The guard checks with the cashier and the manager to see if the customers had simply left their money and tab on the table instead of paying the server. He finds that is indeed the case and disaster is averted.

Let's take another potential trouble spot. In this scenario, the guard constantly walks back and forth by a table of African-American customers, singling them out for observation and making them edgy and nervous. That's a no-no. Guards have to focus on the behavior of a diner, not on their own suspicions. Shadowing or targeting a group, especially on the basis of race or ethnicity, is a violation of our nondiscrimination policy. The guard may think that someone will bolt the restaurant without paying, but it is his or her job to be watchful without making any customers uncomfortable by singling them out for disparate treatment. Remember that the fear that black customers would not pay their checks was at the foundation of many of the cases consolidated under Ridgeway. To single out those guests would be a violation of the consent decree as well as our own policies. So a security guard working for Denny's just can't do that.

This tape is about half an hour long and all our security guards are required to see it before they start work. We've received considerable positive feedback on this. The agencies that handle the guards say that they appreciate the guidance. I think it has helped us cut down on allegations of inappropriate behavior and discourtesy from the security guards, but it's still a little too early to tell, since this is relatively new. Faced with difficult situations in the past, some managers deferred to the police or to security. But managers must manage.

In the videotape example of the diners who supposedly walked out without paying, the tape shows how the incident should have been handled. It also shows what happens when, after checking, the manager and guard determine that the diners have skipped without paying the bill. The correct response is to get the license plate number of the car the people are driving and report it to the authorities.

Because it is the managers who decide what action is needed in the restaurant, the security guards are never to interfere when a manager is talking with a customer. Though the situation may appear, from across the restaurant, as potential trouble, the guard risks making the situation worse by inserting him- or herself in it without the manager's okay.

All this training—the tapes, compliance with the consent decree—doesn't come cheaply. Just to train one of our own people to conduct a training workshop costs about $6,000. Altogether we spend several million dollars each year on compliance and training. We know, however, that we are better off for having spent it. As Joel Gonzales asked of our management participants in the Houston training workshop, "How much is someone's dignity worth?" I won't place a price on human dignity; I don't think anyone else should either.

Procurement: A Fair Share of the Business

he NAACP fair share agreement was already in place when I arrived at Advantica in 1995. One of the things that agreement meant was that Advantica would have to begin boosting the percentage of goods it purchased from minority-owned suppliers. So the effort to find and locate minority vendors was already under way when I came. But it was not a very polished or efficient system, even though it was a first step toward meeting the goal we had signed off on with the NAACP—to have at least 12% of our corporate purchasing come from minority business enterprises. That is a goal that we've met and exceeded, but meeting it was more complex than you might imagine.

Let me give you an example of the type of problem facing the company at the time. You could call it the case of the disappearing shrimp. I won't name this particular vendor. Who knows? He may have gotten his act together in the intervening years, so I wish him well. But shortly before I got here, this supplier wanted to sell Denny's some breaded shrimp. The vendor had a good reputation in the food processing industry because of contracts making food products for the federal government. The vendor had some manufacturing capacity, a certain amount of sophistication, and the willingness to work with us to meet our specifications for breaded shrimp. So Flagstar signed the company to a long-term contract. But there was one problem: The company didn't actually have any shrimp.

Well, you'd be forgiven for asking how Flagstar ended up with a multiyear contract to buy shrimp from a vendor that had no shrimp to sell. The answer is that after the company signed the fair share agreement with the NAACP, it had to move fast, even if, as it turned out, it did not always move wisely. The company ended up feeling pressured to sign up as many minority vendors as quickly as it could. Now all that happened with the shrimp guys was that they agreed to deliver a product they really couldn't deliver. That isn't good. But since they were acting in good faith, it was a relatively minor concern, at least compared to the handful of other companies that approached Flagstar before I arrived. Some of them were found to be fronting for majority-owned corporations. They felt that the company had to present a "black" face to the world after signing the fair share agreement, so they came knocking on the door to help us—and to help themselves, too. The shrimp peddlers, I think, fell more into the category of being too eager and not ready enough to carry out a contract Flagstar rushed into letting them have.

We worked with them for a number of years after I got here, helping them to make good on their contract to deliver the shrimp. This was a family operation, and there were two brothers who actually had a factory, but it just wasn't outfitted with the right equipment to get the shrimp ready. They kept telling us, time after time, that they'd have the equipment ready. They never did get their production facility going. Eventually we had to fulfill our needs by letting this company buy the promised shrimp from a majority-owned company. That is clearly not what we mean by increasing the number of minority companies we do business with. When the contract with the shrimp sellers elapsed in 1997, we didn't renew it.

The company, it was clear, needed someone whose job it was to iron out problems like that and prevent them from arising again, someone to oversee the efforts to bring in minority vendors on more than the haphazard basis that had resulted in the debacle with the shrimp sellers. We needed someone with a vast knowledge of minority business enterprises, legitimate ones, that could do business with Advantica. We needed somebody who could bring routine and order into our minority supplier program, and we needed someone who could join us here in Spartanburg and begin working on these problems immediately. In short, we needed Magaly Petersen-Penn—Maggie—our director of supplier diversity.

So Tell Me—Why Should I Want to Work for You?

In South Carolina, there is an organization called the Carolinas Minority Supplier Development Councils (CMSDC). It is made up of five smaller regional councils in North and South Carolina and includes most of the big employers in both states. So you'll find everything from the drug companies up in the Research Triangle in North Carolina, to the big utilities in both states, to the automobile and automotive parts companies that have come to dot the landscape in South Carolina, like BMW and Michelin. The purpose of these councils is to bring these large corporations together with the smaller minority business enterprises (MBEs) that are looking to expand and secure contracts with the big businesses. In 1995, Dennis Taylor, then our director of purchasing, sat on the executive committee of the council.

Dennis was painfully aware of the problems the company was encountering trying to build a network of minority suppliers, and he was looking for help. He needed that help because this was not his primary area of expertise, and beyond that, Denny's needed to move quickly if it were to find the minority suppliers it needed to meet the fair share agreement. One of the things I was absolutely convinced of when I came aboard was that if Denny's was to seriously increase the number of minority vendors it used, it would have to have someone on staff dedicated solely to that job. If the hiring of minority vendors was a fragmented task, with no single person responsible for it, it was highly likely we would never meet the goals established with the NAACP.

Working on the executive board of the council, Dennis gradually became more and more convinced that one of his fellow board members—Maggie—was the person Denny's and Flagstar needed. Because the council's territory covered two states, many of the officers on the executive committee would have to travel to various meetings. Dennis and Maggie would meet on these sojourns, most often to Charlotte, where the CMSDC met to conduct business. During late 1994 and early 1995, it became clear to Dennis that this was the person for the job at Advantica. Maggie is a tall, elegant Hispanic-American woman with a lilting voice, soft in aspect but serious in purpose. Back then, Maggie was running the minority purchasing program for Michelin North America, here in South Carolina. She had lived in South Carolina for six years, working for Michelin, the big French tire company whose operation is in nearby Greenville, South Carolina. Before that, Maggie had worked in Michelin's headquarters in Lake Success, New York. But because she had been in South Carolina for so many years, she knew the area and the local companies we could draw on. That was a strong point in her favor. Though Michelin would clearly not draw from exactly the same universe of suppliers that we needed, Maggie had experience with a wider range of companies than those that would become vendors to the tire maker. One of the activities that she frequently saw was new companies coming into the CMSDC system to be certified by the councils. That meant she saw how CMSDC gave its stamp of approval to make sure that minority-owned companies were indeed owned by minorities and not fronting for white owners eager to tap into a major company's need for black vendors. Indeed, one of Flagstar's former top procurement executives, Samuel Maw, once told the press that hiring minority vendors was a problem at Denny's: "It is extremely difficult to find them, because they aren't out there."

Well, we needed someone who knew that they were out there and knew where to find them. Dennis thought Maggie was that person, and in retrospect, he has been proven right. But like many of the people who have come to Advantica in the past two or three years, subsequent to my joining the company, she had to do some soul-searching and ask the same questions all of us relative newcomers to Denny's ended up asking: Should I come to work at Advantica? Should I be associated with a company tainted like Denny's? What will my family and friends think? What do I think of myself for doing this?

"A little of that fear of working for Denny's entered into my thinking," she says now. But if you ask Maggie why she decided to leave her relatively comfortable job at Michelin, where she knew what she was doing, to come to Advantica— meaning, of course, to the notorious Denny's—she will give you a straight answer. "But Denny's needed a program to survive, so that would give me a lot of leeway to put something together. I thought I could make a difference."

Maggie came in and talked with our human resources people, just as any other job candidate would do, with Dennis Taylor, and with a few other key executives, before officially joining us in March 1995. I did not make Maggie's acquaintance until after everyone had already signed off and hired her. Needless to say, we've talked to each other many, many times since.

One of the first things that happened after Maggie got here was that the company set up a program to actually identify who was a minority vendor and who was not. Advantica had not taken that step before. Doing this is not as easy as you might think. It necessitates sending out questionnaires to all your suppliers (Figure 8.1). In it, you ask the essential question—who owns you? That survey also asks the source of the products the company uses when it bids on a contract from Advantica. We do this to eliminate middleman fronts, agents, and other third parties who are really getting their products from majority suppliers. It is actually a long and rather tedious process. People don't always want to answer these questions honestly, but typically, they do answer because they want to keep doing business with Denny's.

The exceptions? Every once in a blue moon we find, through other means, some company that does not want to be identified as minority owned. Usually, you know that you are dealing with an MBE because they have been certified as such by local minority supplier councils or by the Small Business Administration. The SBA will also ask questions about ownership to make sure that a company is indeed minority owned: That makes it eligible to seek out any spe-

16. OWNERSHIP CLASSIFICATION:	
☐ American Minority Group	☐ The above company is at least 51% owned and controlled by an American Minority Group.
☐ African American ☐ American Indian ☐ Asian Pacific American ☐ Hispanic American ☐ Other Minority	☐ The above company is at least 51% owned, controlled, and operated by one or more women. ("CONTROL" in this context means exercising the power to make policy decisions. "OPERATE" in this context means being involved actively in the day to day management of the business.) PLEASE ATTACH A COPY OF YOUR SUPPLIER CERTIFICATION (from a Regional Minority Purchasing Council or Approved Equivalent).
☐ Woman Owned ☐ Not Applicable	M/WBE #, if applicable _____
THIS FORM MUST BE SIGNED BY AN OFFICER OF THE FIRM	
I Certify the above information to be true and correct to the best of my knowledge	
OFFICER SIGNATURE:	DATE: NAME & TITLE (PRINT OR TYPE):

Rev. 9/98

Figure 8.1 Advantica's purchasing department requires every potential supplier to complete its Supplier Profile Questionnaire, which asks for gender and racial ownership information. This is an excerpt from that questionnaire.

cial calls for minority bidders from large businesses and to be included in lists of MBEs that a majority-owned company can refer to in order to meet its needs. Yet some MBEs bypass this process altogether. That not only makes it harder for Advantica to meet its goal of 12% minority contracting but also defeats, we think, the ability of the minority-owned business to grow. "Identify yourself as an MBE," Maggie advises the vendor, when she finds one of these companies. "This is a program that will only help you get your foot in the door." But once it's there, the company is judged on its merits, plain and simple.

In early 1995, we had only four minority vendors of any size doing business with us. One of them actually fell into the middleman territory I was speaking of, a company that brokered fresh bread for us in Florida. We have since stopped doing business with them. Another, American Paper Products, is no longer a minority-owned company. Though we had worked with the company to help it pull through financial difficulty, the owner eventually sold the business under financial duress. You'll hear his story a little later. His story is indicative of how hard we can work to help our minority suppliers grow along with us.

Of the original group of minority suppliers, the ones still doing business with us are Quality Croutons in Chicago; Mission Foods, which makes tortillas and nachos for us in California; and Neptune Seafoods, which provides Denny's with breaded shrimp on the west coast. There were perhaps one or two others that have also since fallen by the wayside. At most, there were six minority contractors working with Advantica.

To meet our numbers in the fair share agreement, we had to not only find new MBEs to do business with but also keep some of the original ones going. Let me tell you the story of Harry Pelzer, the former IBM executive who spent years and years trying to keep American Paper Products afloat and keep it a minority supplier for us. American Paper was one of the original MBEs doing business with Advantica when I got here. It sold its products to the Hardee's units we subsequently divested in 1998. What happened to American Paper Products is a story that shows clearly why this part of our business is so important to our future as a company and just as important to the entrepreneurs and employees of the companies who work with us.

They Said, "If You Don't Like It, Start Your Own Business"—So He Did

Turbeville, South Carolina, population 315, is located in Clarendon County, which is not famous for very much, says Pelzer, except for the fact that it is one of the counties that consolidated its fight against school desegregation in the historic 1954 case *Brown v. Board of Education of Topeka*, the one that reached the Supreme Court. Clarendon's population is 60% African-American. The median income for a family of four was only $14,000 in 1993, when Pelzer started American Paper Products there. And the area was not totally unfamiliar to Pelzer, either. Although his parents had migrated north and he had grown up in Philadelphia, Pennsylvania, he is a native of nearby Dorchester County, South Carolina.

So the 10,000-square-foot factory on Route 378 in Turbeville is an important factor in the local economy, a place where farmworkers in the surrounding cucumber fields can trade farm work for factory work, making more money and taking a step up in the world. And it was a big step up for Pelzer, too, who quit his job at IBM in Wilmington, Delaware, in 1985, determined to become an entrepreneur.

"I had an interesting discussion with an IBM executive, trying to explain to him what IBM should do [to best utilize its] minority workforce," says Pelzer. But the supervisor on the other side of the table somehow didn't get it, didn't understand some of the things Pelzer was trying to say in terms of developing at IBM what we have worked on so diligently here—a diverse workforce. Then, says Pelzer, this man said the magic words that eventually had him making paper cups for our former Hardee's division: "If you don't like it, start your own business."

So that's what Pelzer, and a group of his friends, proceeded to do. He began his search by looking for $5.8 million in equity to fund his start-up. But because capital was hard to come by, he ended up getting the business off the ground with only $500,000, most of that being his personal assets and those of some fellow investors. The money was used mostly to lease the factory and the two machines that made the paper cups that was American Paper Products' main commodity. "It was the classic bootstrap" says Pelzer.

In early 1995, Pelzer's company was up and running, supplying paper cups to Hardee's, when we still owned restaurants in that chain. Things were apparently going well for him—so well, in fact, that he was invited in early 1995 to give an address at a meeting of the Foothills Minority Supplier Development Council that I attended. I heard his story and was impressed and went up to him after the speech. I told him how happy I was that he was doing business with us. I also told him that if there was anything he ever needed, he should give us a call.

Well, that call came not long after. Harry let it be known that his company had hit the wall. He had used up all the money he had on the start-up phase, and American Paper Products wouldn't be in any condition to supply cups to us, or even to meet his modest payroll for its 42 employees, unless he received some help—and fast.

So one summer day he drove up to Spartanburg, and in my conference room he sat down with me, with Ray Hood-Phillips, and with Dennis Taylor. It wasn't a long meeting, maybe an hour, tops. But Harry explained that his company was running out of cash and would no longer exist if he didn't get some help soon. So I made the commitment that we would lend him money on a monthly basis. Over the next year we advanced American Paper Products about $350,000, lending them about a tenth of that each month. That money enabled them to buy raw products and make their payroll—at which point they'd deliver the cups to Hardee's, we'd pay them for the goods, and they would repay our loan to them.

Pelzer said later that I understood what he needed because I'm a turnaround executive—that I was working to create shareholder value at Flagstar and knew how to devise an investment that would help his company when he needed it—in this case, a revolving loan facility for a worthwhile company that could not find other financing. We spoke mainly numbers that afternoon while Ray and some of our financial people were there. Sure, it probably would have been a lot simpler—and certainly cheaper—to dismiss American Paper Products and buy our cups from some mainstream supplier without start-up problems. But that wasn't the point. Not only would that have hindered us in meeting our goals but I would have been disappointed in it, too.

I am very flattered by Harry's description of me and happy to be able to report that we were able to maintain a supplier relationship with American Paper Products until the sale of our Hardee's fast-food division. But while those 42 men and women are still happily working at the Turbeville factory, their future may be endangered. Pelzer decided that he just couldn't make it on his own. In September 1998, he sold his company to a majority-owned firm, Dopaco. That the company has survived in any form at all, says Pelzer, is due to Flagstar's quick intervention. But Pelzer says he is worried that Dopaco may move the jobs in his factory out of tiny Turbevillle, leaving 42 workers out of their jobs.

Pelzer, too, has had a hard time trying to make a go of it with his company. This is a man, after all, who came home from work one day and told his wife, "Honey, I want to quit IBM and go sell paper cups." Okay, so I don't know if those were his exact words. But the point is that as hard as conducting this business was for him, his wife, and their children, Harry is still the type of guy who believes in his mission of economic empowerment—and worries about his employees.

"There's a guy who works for me named Walter," says Pelzer. "Four and a half years ago he was picking cucumbers in a field. Now he's my top maintenance guy, taking care of sophisticated electrical and mechanical equipment, which is computer based. We took guys like Walter and turned them into people who are able to take care of machinery like that."

Since its inception, American Paper Products has also increased its customer base; it now sells cups to McDonald's as well. People like Walter, Harry says, may be out of work again if Dopaco relocates the facility, consolidating it with some of its other paper products factories in North Carolina. But if that happens, we will at least take some comfort in knowing that Advantica, as a company dedicated to helping develop minority suppliers, has made a real difference in South Carolina for Walter and all the people like him. I'm proud of the economic development our minority purchasing program has started. It's one of the aspects of turning around Denny's that people don't always see (Figure 8.2).

Figure 8.2 Jim Adamson, left, received the 1996 National Association for the Advancement of Colored People CEO of the Year Award from Kweisi Mfume, president and chief executive officer of the NAACP. (Photo courtesy of George Frye.)

If Apple Computer Got Started in a Garage, Why Can't I Boil Syrup in Mom's Basement?

One of the things Maggie had to do when she arrived here was to make sure the purchasing agents included MBEs in the contracting process. To that end, the purchasing agents—the people who actually draw up the specifications for contracts and are the first contact between the company and the vendors—had to take direct responsibility for increasing the number of minority vendors.

Since 1995, the number of purchasing agents has fluctuated—depending on the number of restaurant chains under the corporate umbrella—from six to nine. No matter how many there are, though, Maggie has implemented one big rule. When we set a contract out for bid (we call them RFPs, or requests for proposals), whoever is responsible for the product we want to buy through that contract has to consult with Maggie to see whether there were any MBEs who ought to get the opportunity as well.

The purchasing agents were receptive to this idea, and not just because Denny's had signed a fair share agreement or because I had come determined to make the company a fair and inclusive place. The old complaint that MBEs are just not out there to be found simply doesn't cut it anymore. These companies are too eager, and work too quickly, for that to be a useful excuse. Some of our suppliers have managed to overcome pretty tough odds to become successful businesses before we even heard of them, so it didn't ring true when past employees said that they can't find them. Besides, sometimes they find us. Michele Hoskins spent 18 months trying to do just that. This is a woman whose story I find impressive—even before she ended up with a $3 million annual contract to sell syrup to Denny's in 1995.

Hoskins's company, Michele Foods, is located in suburban Chicago and makes syrups—maple, honey crème, and butter pecan. Michele Foods was already a successful business before its owner started calling Denny's purchasing department. Hoskins grew up watching her mother whip up batches of an old family recipe for honey butter syrup, one she says has been passed down in her family, mother to daughter, since the days of slavery. Now, liking an old family recipe is one thing, but making a business out of it is something else. That was something Hoskins didn't really consider until she was facing a divorce in the late 1970s and looking for more money than she had to support her two children.

Hoskins, however, didn't actually have the recipe for the syrup from which she would build her business. Family tradition mandated that only the third daughter would learn the secret recipe from her mother. Michele was daughter number two. It took some convincing, but eventually her mother passed on the secret recipe to Michele. Hoskins has told people, "As soon as she gave me the recipe, all my entrepreneurial spirit came out. I thought, 'This is my business.'"

Well, the young woman found out that starting a business is a tough game. When she started out in 1982, she found another company in Chicago that would commercialize her recipe—for a price, of course. Soon Hoskins had sold her car, her furniture, and ultimately her condo in pursuit of her dream. The college-educated Hoskins had long quit her teaching job at a Catholic elementary school to pursue the syrup company idea full time. She ended up living with her kids in the attic of her mother's house, mixing and pouring bottles of syrup in the basement. At one point, she even was on welfare. Altogether, by the time she had enough syrup in bottles to start selling it to local stores in Chicago, she was out $150,000. "Everybody thought I had lost my mind," she said.

But like any entrepreneur, she stuck with it (no pun intended) and eventually became successful, first getting her syrups into the local mom-and-pop stores in Chicago before landing the big contract in 1984 to sell to Jewel Foods—a major food chain—especially those in black neighborhoods. Just when she'd finally been given a chance, another problem emerged: Her biggest customer had just ordered 672 cases of syrup, but going down to Mom's basement and taking 45 minutes to pour syrup into bottles for just one case meant three weeks of solid syrup pouring—without time to eat, sleep, or go to the bathroom—to meet the order. Clearly there had to be a better way, and there was. Hoskins found a company that would do the bottling for her in a real production facility. Then other orders followed, until her breakthrough in 1992, when an investor put up the $300,000 she needed to start selling Michele Foods syrups nationally.

So why would a woman who had accomplished all of that, who was selling her goods in major supermarket chains like Jewel and Dominick's in Chicago, Winn-Dixie in the South, and Kroger in the Midwest, have to beg to get an appointment to sell syrup to Denny's? Well, from what she says, that's just about what she had to do, calling repeatedly and sending letters to Flagstar's purchasing department.

In an early press report about her first encounters with the company, Hoskins said, "When I first called Flagstar, someone told me the company couldn't buy from me because it had a deal in the works with Log Cabin. I said 'You'll give me a better explanation than that.'"

I don't think Michele Hoskins ever got a realistic explanation to her question. But once I arrived and after Maggie came to work with us, we looked at the information we had on her and decided to do business with her. Today Michele Foods is a $7.5 million business that continues to grow. In the fall of 1998, it signed a cross-promotion deal with General Mills. The promotion urged consumers to use its Bisquick baking mix for pancakes—and add a little Michele's Honey Crème on top. We are pleased to be a part of the growth of Michele's company.

A Contract Is Not Always Simple

Sometimes finding a minority business enterprise that can do what you want really is tough. For example: If you're looking for a single minority-owned business in the entire nation that makes frozen french fried potatoes, you'll look in vain. (If I'm wrong, and you know of such a company, call Maggie!) When a company comes knocking at your door, finding it isn't going to be hard, as long as you're listening for the knock. Sometimes, however, you have to go out and search—something Maggie does very well. She knows a great deal about many of these companies because of her previous position at Michelin and through her contacts with the various minority supplier councils around the country. The National Minority Supplier Development Council (NMSDC), headquartered in New York City, has a convention every year. It is made up of 38 regional councils, including the Carolinas council, in which we are active.

Then there are the regional conventions and fairs of the councils, which are a major source of referrals and contacts as well. We make it a point to send someone to the larger events in Chicago and Los Angeles, as well as the one for the state of South Carolina. In addition, within the NMSDC, there is a group of companies that operate in the food service group; they swap ideas and sources and contacts with each other. There's also the wonderful resource of the NMSDC database, which includes 16,000 minority-owned businesses in the United States. So from all these sources, Maggie passes on information to the purchasing agents whose job it is to make sure our suppliers are as diverse as the rest of our company.

Now including MBEs among the companies that bid on Advantica's goods is par for the course. Part of the reason for this is certainly that we feel it's the right thing to do. But another part is that there's no longer a real excuse not to include minority vendors—they're almost always out there. For any given bid, the RFP in question will go out to between three and six vendors. It's a rule here that one of them has to be a minority-owned company. That means that right now, for any contract put out to bid by any unit of Advantica, the chances are between 15% and 33.3% that an MBE will be awarded the job. That's a far cry from the days when we had only a handful of minority companies working with us. Altogether now we have 29 major contracts with MBEs. In 1998, they did $120 million in business with us.

What's a major contract? One that calls for a total of more than $100,000 in goods—so those 29 firms exclude minor expenditures. A restaurant manager who buys a few wreaths and a Christmas tree to decorate his or her restaurant is fine as far as it goes. But it doesn't go nearly far enough. For the record, our purchasing decisions are binding on company-owned restaurants but not on the franchisees. They can use their judgment in finding suppliers, as long as they meet the specifications that we demand to maintain consistent quality at all Denny's restaurants. But clearly, many of them find it easier to follow our recommendations than to reinvent the wheel in terms of purchasing products.

Our largest minority vendor, Siméus Foods, has an interesting history. It used to belong to us. One of the things we've done since I arrived is cut down on the number of businesses that the corporation owns. We've had to get rid of some of the service businesses and captive suppliers we owned to reduce our debt and focus our attention and resources on restaurant operations. So we have sold off all but our core operations—Denny's, El Pollo Loco, Coco's, and Carrows. Among the businesses we sold was one of the companies that Flagstar had owned for many years—Portion-Trol Foods. Portion-Trol processed raw beef into the hamburger patties, chicken-fried steaks, and other meat products used in our restaurants.

At about the same time that we hired Peter Schwab from Ernst & Young to find us a buyer for Portion-Trol, there was a Haitian-born businessman, Dumas Siméus, who was interested in puchasing a company. Siméus, who had lived in Connecticut, had gotten to know the food processing business while working alongside the late Reginald Lewis, one of the pathbreaking African-American businesspeople in this country. He was famous for building up Beatrice TLC, a company that had revenues of $2 billion at its height. Beatrice was privately held and many of its operations were overseas.

Siméus had been president of Beatrice Foods Latin America. It was there, working for one of the country's richest men, that he developed the desire to become an entrepreneur, not a manager. With no hard feelings, he left Beatrice in 1992 and sought the financing to buy a company in the food processing industry: "I had watched Reg and seen how things were done and wanted to move on. I didn't want to work for anyone anymore."

To find the company he wanted, Siméus hooked up with an old friend, Don Lawhorne, who was president and chief executive of the MESBIC Ventures Holding Company, a Dallas-based investment fund looking to back minority businesses. Lawhorne had so much faith in Siméus that he convinced the Haitian immigrant to pick up stakes and relocate to Dallas from Connecticut to carry out his search for a company he could call his own.

The two of them spent hours together in Dallas, meeting people who could finance whatever deal they might bring to them, connecting with brokers and other middlemen who might be selling a company they'd be interested in buying. I guess it may have struck some people as odd, the white guy with the Southern accent squiring around an internationally traveled businessman, an impeccably dressed immigrant with that slight French accent from the islands. But there they were, driving Dallas's endless freeways, looking for the right company. During the first few months of 1995 that Siméus was in Dallas, he and Lawhorne said they must have seriously considered buying 80 to 100 different companies. When Lawhorne, through his contacts, found out that Portion-Trol was up for sale, it seemed that this was just the kind of company the two men hoped to buy.

To buy it, however, they needed the help of our company at two critical junctures. When an intermediary decides to sell a company for a client—and in this case, the client was us—they are interested in getting the highest price. One of the things they do to ensure that is to make any prospective buyers go through an exhaustive round of bidding. The seller's representatives have to meet some of the prospective buyers—at least the ones they take most seriously—and do their due diligence, checking out reputation, management, and finances.

Lawhorne and Siméus had lined up Citicorp Venture Capital (CVC) to finance the equity part of the deal. At the last minute, however, CVC reneged on its pledge to come up with the money. A company as prestigious as Citicorp certainly would have made it easier for them to line up the bank loans they'd need to complete the purchase of Portion-Trol. Without equity financing, however, there would be no deal at all. So Lawhorne and Siméus scrambled to get alternative financing. They showed up in Spartanburg a few days later in August 1996 to talk with Paul Wexler, Advantica's executive vice president of procurement. The two men worked desperately to convince Paul that they could indeed find more equity financing to replace that of CVC. Usually, when a major partner like that falls out, it kills any chance for a deal. But Paul already had talked to me about the situation, so he let them know their alternate financing would be fine. That okay made them a major contender among the bidders looking to buy the company.

I didn't have to take a direct role in helping Siméus buy Portion-Trol until the final meeting of the bankers to approve the financing. Now I wasn't there in person, and like a lot of these meetings, the atmosphere was tense. What was the weather like outside? Was it raining? No one could tell you, because they were all too deeply involved in a crucial meeting hosted by Siméus and Lawhorne in Dallas—a meeting that would ultimately decide whether Portion-Trol went to a minority owner. A total of perhaps three dozen to four dozen bankers from around the country had flown into Dallas, converging that day at the Hyatt Hotel near the Dallas–Ft. Worth International Airport.

I did attend the meeting via a conference call, trying to explain to these bankers why they should loan $55 million to a foreign-born business executive and a native Southerner who wanted to do right by him. Siméus can remember vividly that race had nothing to do with this transaction. These bankers only wanted to know one thing, he recalled: "How would they get their money back? 'Lots of people pay lip service to diversity,' one of them said. 'How can we be sure you won't screw this little guy and we're left holding the bag?'"

It was a long meeting that started early. First, all the principals made their presentations. Then Siméus and Lawhorne made their pitch, speaking of their vision for the company, and how they would grow it. Paul Wexler was there too, emphasizing a few points that he hoped would sway the bankers, who were worried that lending their money to a company that had only one customer—us—was too risky a move. Paul told the assembled bankers that this company had been founded specifically to supply food to Denny's and all the rest of our units, so that we would not suddenly go elsewhere to meet our needs for these products.

I talked briefly to that room full of anonymous people, and I added something that I now see as crucial in trying to build a network of minority-owned suppliers. I told the bankers that if they would loan Siméus the money to buy Portion-Trol, not only would we extend a five-year contract worth $100 million per year but we would also do it on a "take-or-pay" basis. That means we would pay that money to Siméus even if we didn't buy any goods from our former captive subsidiary. That, indeed, would give the banks an almost ironclad guarantee that they would get their money back. That clinched the deal.

It takes, as it always does in these matters, a few months to get all the paperwork together, but on September 27, 1996, we closed on the sale of Portion-Trol and created Siméus Foods, our largest minority-owned supplier. With our contract in hand, Siméus could gear up for production with other chains, and that's what Siméus has done. The company now has contracts to supply beef and other food-stuffs to other restaurant chains, including the Olive Garden, Red Lobster, Church's, and Popeye's.

* * * * * *

To seriously boost economic development within the African-American, Latino, and other minority communities, we need to deal in larger numbers. The 29 minority companies that I've talked about here did $120 million worth of business with us. In addition, our majority suppliers did $5 million on what we call a "second-tier" initiative. This $125 million total amounts to over 15% of the $664 million that we spent in 1998 on all our vendors.

To understand what a second-tier vendor is, you have to understand a little about the RFPs we put out to potential vendors; you also need to understand the language used in them, language that we've made very specific in the last few years. A second-tier vendor is, in lay terms, a subcontractor. It is a way for us to employ minority talent when we cannot find an MBE to act as a prime contractor. But unlike the unclear situation we had here in 1994, all of us now understand who's who, and how they've come to work for Denny's, or any other Advantica restaurant subsidiary, because it's now clearly spelled out in the contracts we use.

Until 1997 or so, our contract language was pretty standard. We certainly let it be known that we wanted a certain quantity of chicken wings or hash browns or whatever to be delivered by a particular date and at a particular price. After Maggie came aboard to oversee and develop our program of minority vendors, we changed the language so that all of our bidders would realize that we are serious and committed to using minority-owned businesses. The contract makes it clear that if a majority-owned company wants to do business with Denny's, then it also will have to do a significant share of business with an MBE—or tell us why. In actuality, the language is a little more legal than that. But that's essentially what we're saying to the world these days. We put it into our contracts so that our commitment to diversity is clear and unmistakable.

We also state specifically that the reason we want to include minority-owned businesses in all our contracts is that such inclusion is good not only for the vendor but, in the long term, for Advantica, too. By supporting minority-controlled companies, we are recycling money into the communities in which we operate. That sounds fair to me. And because we put forth these propositions while soliciting bids, everyone, from civil rights groups to our own people and everyone in between, knows that we are serious.

Primary contractors know that when they send in a bid that they are doing so on our terms—which, explicitly stated, means that we expect them to make their best effort at using an MBE in their operations or explain to us why this is not possible. All companies chosen to contract with Advantica have to report quarterly to our staff on their progress in using an MBE during the life of their contract, or we can consider that they have broken the terms of that contract.

In addition, we lay out in that contract how the majority-owned company can earn credit for using an MBE in its operations and supplying its products to Advantica. This is important to us, because we want to avoid the same old problem of counting some marginal business practice as making a contribution to what we are really after: serious economic development. A majority contractor may be able to say that it cannot find a second-tier supplier in a particular business, and that may be certifiably true. But that does not mean that we will allow the company to use an African-American who, for instance, does minor landscaping for them twice a year as an excuse or as a substitute for not doing more.

Though our contract language encourages the majority contractor to utilize MBEs as second-tier suppliers, our numbers are pretty specific about how those MBEs can be used. When the purchasing analysis is done on a bid after we get it back, we make it clear that if this company is going to do business with us, it has to meet a percentage level or there is no deal between the prime contractor and Advantica.

Part of the analysis is to determine exactly what that percentage is and how we expect it to be met. In some cases, depending on the product and what part of the country it is coming from, we will say that as much as 25% of the value of the bid must be done through MBEs. But that is on the high side of the scale. Usually we insist on between 5% and 15% of the business going that way. When the vendor comes to us once every three months to let us know how it is doing in meeting these goals, we caucus to see if there is anything we can do to help the vendor. We want to help because we are basing this whole program on enlightened self-interest, not hostility, and not on proving some sense of moral superiority. Yes, we are doing the right thing. But you can't do the right thing alone; you need other people to help, and you can't be successful at it if you're obnoxious about it with the very people who can help you meet your goals.

This is how we get minority suppliers into the pipeline. It was, however, one of the last parts of our program to be developed. First, we had to make sure we had a working system for dealing with all of our first-tier minority suppliers before we could start going to the majority-owned suppliers and saying that they, too, would have to work with the minority companies. After all, how could we tell them who to work with—or who not to—unless we were pretty sure ourselves that we had some names to hand over and some help to offer?

Remember that I said we haven't yet identified any minority-owned company that makes french fries? Do we give up on that? No way. Our french fry contract right now is with Lamb-Weston, one of the world's largest frozen potato processors. It's a division of ConAgra, the giant agricultural company based in Omaha, Nebraska. We do about $14 million in business each year with Lamb-Weston. Since by contract we have set a level of MBE participation with them at 5%, we feel that we have to help them meet that goal. Right now the company is between 3% and 4% on its contract in terms of using minority businesses. Determining how to meet these goals is a complex process, because some companies believe they have the right to count some of the minorities they use in other aspects of their general business toward credit with the specific contract they have with Advantica. Some of this we allow. So they will call us for advice, and our diversity vendor program can tell them where they can go to find janitorial services or where they can find a MBE in the paper and packaging business. We never make them, or anybody else for that matter, use any specific vendor. But we have things worked out well enough with the companies we do business with so that when they need to find an MBE to help them meet their obligations, they feel that they can call us. To have a partner with that attitude is not to be underestimated. Having a vendor with that attitude also makes us more amenable to renewing our contract with them when that time comes. If we are working with people who understand what we are trying to do with minority businesses, then we look favorably upon them at contract renewal time.

In terms of getting MBEs that are first-tier contractors, we have to realize that a lot of these companies, though far from all of them, are still small businesses, not just minority businesses. And with that reality comes all of the problems of any other small business. The difference, I think, is that small businesses that are owned by whites often have some secondary resources they can count on when they get into trouble, whereas many minority-based enterprises do not. To the best of our ability, then, we will help them out, just as we will help out some of our minority-owned franchisees to get the correct financing, or just about anything else that they need.

It's not too difficult to realize that in running thousands of restaurants, we have to use a certain number of french fries or eggs or paper towels. But you might be surprised at some of the other things that we have to buy. It might not come immediately to mind, for instance, that Denny's and all the Advantica restaurants have to have first-aid kits. (Let me hasten to add that no, our restaurants are not hotbeds of workers' compensation cases!) Working in kitchens and restaurants, there will inevitably be burned fingers, scraped elbows, and other minor injuries. That's why we need to have a first-aid kit in every restaurant in our system. It was an opportunity that a smart businessman named Sylvester Formey took advantage of, and one that I believe is very typical of how we make ourselves known to minority suppliers.

Formey's company is located in Savannah, Georgia. Vanguard Distributors is a certified MBE affiliated with the Georgia Minority Suppliers Development Council, one of those 38 regional councils that Maggie makes a point of getting to know. And Advantica is also one of the corporate planners represented on that board. Vanguard is a relatively small company with about 10 employees and one factory. I don't think its revenues total more than $10 million per year. Yet in 1997, Formey called Maggie cold and asked, "How do I become an Advantica vendor?" She sent him the supplier profile questionnaire we send any company that wants to become a vendor for us. Then we notified the purchasing agent in charge of buying first-aid kits that we had found this small minority business, a distributor of industrial safety products that wanted to sell first-aid kits to Advantica. The purchasing agent sent Vanguard the basic RFP we had going out on first-aid products.

The questionnaire asks the basic questions about how big the company is, where its processing or manufacturing facilities are located, and who owns the company. We ask specifically if a company is geographically limited in its distribution abilities or whether it can easily deliver its products to any part of the country. We ask to see the business's credit report. (Vanguard's, by the way, was rated as good by one business rating company.) We even make sure that a company new to us has the requisite amount of liability insurance. Who knows when a Denny's customer will come into contact with a product that somehow proves unsound or unsafe?

Asking questions like this might seem like common sense. But we didn't always do it when I first came here. There were bids that were accepted on the basis of history, or on the basis of a gut feeling, or on the basis of fear that Advantica had to sign someone up as a minority vendor or else. But the organized survey of what minority-owned businesses actually did, which would be based on information like this, seemed to be available on only a haphazard basis— sometimes it was there; sometimes it wasn't. Sometimes we paid attention to it, sometimes we didn't. We are, needless to say, more rigorous now.

As a result, when Vanguard sent in its reply to our purchasing people, they had all the information they needed to make a decision. Since they liked what they found, the business's owner, Sylvester Formey, and his company got the contract, which in 1998 was worth $220,000, supplying the first-aid kits in all of our restaurants. It's not a long-term contract of the sort we have found so effective in building up our minority vendors, but it is a start. Some vendors, like Sylvester Formey and Michele Hoskins, will specifically seek out Denny's on their own. But we realize that that won't always be the case. We'll still have to go looking for companies ourselves, either because we want to help out a first-tier contractor or because we want to keep faith with our internal policy of finding at least one potential minority bidder for each bid we send out.

So as you might imagine, in addition to having our people go to the minority supplier council fairs and conventions, Advantica is also involved in that old standby, advertising. Yes, we did it before; yes, we do even more of it now. You may see an ad for us in, say, *Black Enterprise* magazine. We hope we can feature a success story, like Michele Hoskins's story, and use it to draw in other minority-owned businesses that might never have thought of selling to Denny's (Figure 8.3). I've heard some people say they're a little surprised to see Denny's advertising to recruit African-American and other minority vendors. How brazen! How could they! the thinking goes. It is neither brazen nor insulting nor disrespectful, especially if you believe that we've changed—and we have. Maggie likes to joke that ultimately, Advantica won't need anybody like her after a few more years. The process will be so well defined, so smoothly run, that the MBEs among Denny's already diverse supplier base will account for far more than the current 18.8% of our contracts. That is already more than one-half higher than the 12% we agreed to in the fair share agreement. We reached that level in 1996 ... and revised it to 13% for 1997–2000. We're especially proud of those numbers in light of the fact that the average U.S. company awards only 4% of its business to minority suppliers. It is numbers like these that show we mean business when it comes to diversifying our vendors and suppliers.

Figure 8.3 Michele Hoskins was featured in a Denny's print ad, created by The Chisholm–Mingo Group, that appeared in black publications.

Our Franchisees Take Us Forward

We've worked hard to convince African-Americans and other people of color that Denny's wants them as customers, that we respect their patronage. We've had to work just as hard, though, to convince them that we want them as business partners. We believe that owning a Denny's franchise represents another chance for all minorities to become part of the Advantica family—and to own a profitable business.

In Flagstar's discussions with the NAACP, the ones that resulted in the fair share agreement, it quickly became clear that Denny's would have to boost the number of its minority franchise owners if we were to regain the credibility we lost during the early 1990s. Prior to the NAACP agreement, there had been only one black franchisee with Denny's. He had built his restaurant in 1992 in the Watts section of Los Angeles, to great acclaim. For two years it was successful, with a menu that combined traditional Southern African-American cuisine, such as greens and chitlins, with the usual Denny's breakfasts, lunches, and dinners. Not only was it one of the few places in the neighborhood to offer local residents a decent place to eat but it was also one of the trickle of new investments in the Watts-Willowbrook neighborhood since the 1965 riots. The restaurant also offered jobs to dozens of people in the neighborhood who otherwise might never have found employment. The local press called the place Denny's N the Hood, a parody of the title of filmmaker John Singleton's *Boyz N the Hood*.

But by 1994, that franchise was in financial trouble. The owner apparently couldn't meet the rent in the shopping mall in which the restaurant was located. The franchisee also failed to meet the terms of a government loan he had taken out to build the restaurant, according to county officials interviewed at the time. Ultimately, Denny's had to move in very quickly when the restaurant was shuttered in the fall of 1994. To save the jobs and keep the community goodwill this place had generated, Denny's quickly agreed to take it over, moving in and reopening it only days after creditors closed its doors. That was an unfortunate circumstance. But today, we remain committed to this area of Los Angeles and another minority franchisee is interested in building a second Denny's restaurant in Watts.

The fact that few African-Americans owned a Denny's franchise when I arrived was a stark contrast to the situation at other major franchise operations, especially in the fast-food industry. McDonald's, for instance, had 12 black franchise owners as far back as 1972, enough for them to organize into the National Black McDonald's Operators

Association, a group whose numbers have continued to grow.

At Burger King, the company signed a covenant with Operation PUSH back in 1983 to increase minority-owned franchises. Burger King renewed that commitment in 1991, when the company said it would aim to increase the number of minority-owned franchises by 1% annually through the turn of the century. By 1998, about one-third of all Burger King franchises around the world were minority owned. The number-three fast-food business, Wendy's, has gone on record as trying to attract more minority franchise holders, especially in their push to open up restaurants in central-city neighborhoods.

Yes, these companies did what they did, to varying degrees, in response to pressure from outside their companies. But what they did also made sense. In the late twentieth-century United States, your customer base in virtually any part of the country is sure to be a rainbow; it won't be very long before, according to census forecasts, the "minority" is a majority. Already by 1990, according to the U.S. Census, people of color were in the majority in 51 of the nation's 200 largest cities. That trend is not expected to reverse itself. So it's inconsistent and foolish to broaden your customer base while making no effort to evolve from having a mostly white group of franchise owners.

We aim to remedy that. I don't believe that most of our black customers are aware of the number of Denny's franchises owned by African-Americans or other people of color. But our research indicates that it does make a difference to many of our African-American guests whether the restaurant in which they eat is black owned. Not everybody cares, but there are undoubtedly customers who are eager to "buy black" and are keenly aware of whether they are patronizing a black-owned establishment. Beyond that, whether people of any color choose one restaurant over another has more to do with the basics: whether they'll be treated respectfully, whether they'll get good food at a fair price, and whether they'll have an enjoyable time when they sit down to eat.

Nevertheless, adding more minority franchise owners would be a clear sign that the company was serious not only about repairing its image but also about becoming the diverse, inclusive corporation we at Advantica want to be. After all, it's not just African-Americans who are upset about what's gone on at Denny's in the past. I have heard white people, too, say that they would not patronize Denny's because of its treatment of minority customers.

I won't deny there was some thought that simply having more black owners in the system could make those particular restaurants, as well as Denny's as a whole, more sensitive about how to treat all its customers. And the better that African-American customers are treated, the more often they'll come to eat. That's good for our image and good for our business, as well as the right thing to do. Moreover, franchise owners, essentially being entrepreneurs, have a big interest in making sure that their operations are run correctly. After all, they've put their own money and a lot of hard work into these businesses.

As the number of minority-owned franchises increased from the early 1990s, the number of minority customers has gone up too. Currently, minorities own and operate roughly 40% of Denny's franchises. That's 309 of 823 restaurants. (The other 800-plus Denny's are company owned.) Of those 309 restaurants, in early 1999, 119 were owned by African-Americans, 30 had Latino owners, and 43 were owned by Asian-Pacific Americans. The balance of the minority franchisees are of Middle Eastern, East Indian, and Native American background. All of those numbers are up substantially from when I came in the midst of the troubles.

I don't think there is necessarily a direct correlation between the number of black people eating in our restaurants and the number owning them. But I don't think those two figures are entirely unrelated, either. As we make Denny's into a more inclusive place, it's just inevitable that there will be some carryover toward a diverse ownership base. The increasing number of African-American customers might have occurred on its own, without steps to specifically expand the number of minority franchise owners. But there was no reason to leave that to chance. I certainly had no desire to do so, and the company's fair share agreement with the NAACP is essentially a moral covenant. The civil rights group makes the pact with corporations on a moral basis; no one wants, expects, or plans legal action to make it work.

Fred Rasheed, the former director of economic development for the NAACP, helped negotiate the fair share agreement with the company before I arrived. He'd be the first to say that it took a while for that covenant to make itself felt.

"Initially, after we signed the agreement," he said in an interview, "we met with Flagstar two, three times a year to monitor their progress. We had some pretty pointed monitoring agreements in franchising. Some of the people there weren't excited about any of it. There were a few people who were not excited about the franchise agreement, as well as the whole agreement. You can learn a lot about a corporation by what gets done and what doesn't get done."

Rasheed, who helped negotiate some 40 fair share agreements, left the NAACP in 1995 to start his own marketing and consulting business. He remembered that no one would come right out and say they weren't going to comply with any of the fair share commitments—though he didn't hesitate to add that some other companies around the country do just that.

"When you have a company with that many restaurants, which employ that many people, you just cannot monitor every single incident. You have to establish strong policies and rules, and [the employees] know that if they stray, they'll be punished." Rasheed also thought our company's lack of advertising during the early years of the agreement cost us speedy advancement toward our goal of more minority franchisees.

"It is [often] very hard to get companies to utilize black media," he said. "Even today it's hard." Well, that isn't hard for us anymore, if it ever was. In addition to the $13 million we spend annually to reach minority consumers, we also use minority publications to reach potential minority franchisees. Denny's wants a more diverse set of franchisees. So you're more likely now to see an advertisement for opportunities at Denny's in the pages of *Jet*, *Ebony*, or *Black Enterprise* magazines than in *The Wall Street Journal*. It wasn't that Denny's never looked for franchise owners in these places—it's just that we didn't do it often enough to get our name out there, to persuade people that we were serious. For all these reasons, I set as one of my priorities the creation of a process that would allow Denny's franchise system to become more reflective of America.

A Burger King Connection Comes through Again

To give us the best shot at meeting that goal, Denny's needed somebody talented and ambitious to be in charge of franchise development. Although we already had someone in charge of franchise development when I came to the company, John Romandetti, Denny's president, wanted a fresh face for the position after he arrived. He determined that we needed someone with plenty of experience dealing with attracting new franchise operators in general. The person would be committed to expanding our franchise base into minority communities and wouldn't be put off by the very peculiar, high-visibility situation in which our company found itself. Building a franchise system is one thing, but building one in the face of unrelenting public cynicism, the threat of severe financial troubles at the parent company level, and the distrust of many of your potential customers is another. By late 1996, John had already asked an executive search firm to come up with a short list of candidates who would fit the bill.

Among the names on the list was Jim Lyons, a Burger King executive. Flagstar, of course, had already hired three former high-ranking managers from Burger King: Craig Bushey, John Romandetti, and Ray Hood-Phillips. Since John had worked with Jim Lyons before and respected the work he had done for Burger King in franchise development, Jim came to Denny's attention now with some things already in his favor. Though there were certainly other names on that list that let us know exactly what talent was out there, John really wanted Jim. But the question was, would he come?

In the spring of 1997, John, who lives in Arizona, interviewed Jim at the Phoenix Airport. Our company flew Jim out there from Burger King headquarters in Miami, so that the new president of Denny's could answer Jim's questions and let him know why he was wanted and what he would be expected to do. From what they tell me now, it wasn't an easy sell. There's no reason we should have expected it to be otherwise. Even though we all knew each other from Burger King, where Jim had spent 14 years working with franchisees and straightening out some of the problems that arose, Denny's was still, well, Denny's. Its reputation was what it was, and frankly, Jim didn't want to come. Not only was the prospect of joining Denny's a daunting one, but Jim had risen nicely through the ranks at Burger King, where he was vice president of franchising and development services when Denny's came calling.

In Phoenix, the two men talked for hours. John listened carefully to what Jim was asking. One of the big things Jim wanted to know was how management planned to turn the organization around so that Denny's would be attractive to franchisees. John agreed that there were challenges but pointed out the ways in which Denny's planned to grow. John also spent time telling Jim about the strategies they hoped to use to improve Denny's franchise development. John had been dissatisfied with our recent efforts to grow the number of franchises.

The two men also talked about the financial structure of the company. We were still known as Flagstar then, and our business was being hurt by the poor performance of our Hardee's restaurants, which were fast losing market share to Burger King and Wendy's. John went to great pains to reassure him. As it turned out, when our company subsequently entered chapter 11, our franchise operations were not seriously affected. Indeed, it has turned out that franchising has represented one of Advantica's main paths of growth.

Those were just some of the questions that floated that day in the hot, dry Arizona air. It was the back-and-forth discussion of two seasoned professionals. Perhaps the hottest question was what Denny's response would be to the litany of racial woes it faced. Was it possible, Jim Lyons wanted to know, to actually attract minority franchisees in light of Denny's reputation? And if it was, was the company really prepared to offer them opportunities to make money and grow? In short, Denny's was asking Jim to leave a secure position, where he had mastered the art of keeping franchisees happy, and where he had already begun to build the very minority franchise presence Denny's now wanted. Denny's wanted him to leave success and to take a chance on a turnaround situation. That was asking a lot.

It was the turnaround aspect of all this, I believe, plus the chance to grow the company and work with people he knew, that finally convinced Jim to join Denny's in leading our franchise development. He saw that Flagstar, in early 1996, very much resembled in some respects the Burger King of 1992. Burger King was never in quite as precarious a position as Flagstar was—but it was facing some financial problems and had problems developing the market share it wanted. Burger King was trying to reposition itself, or, more accurately, trying to find its position in the market, though Burger King's problems had much more to do with the food it sold than the way it treated its customers.

Jim also admitted to a certain comfort level he expected to find at our company, after having worked with John and me. So in May 1996, Jim and his family left south Florida and joined us in Spartanburg. It's a far reach from France, where Jim was born. But just as my father did, Jim's father worked with the military, and thus Jim had lived all over the world. In some sense, coming to a small town in South Carolina was just a throwback to the days when he was constantly stepping off planes in different countries as his family moved around. Jim has a positive attitude, and it has helped him to expand a professionally run franchise development operation that is strong, responsive, profitable and, not least of all, inclusive and diverse.

He's done a good job. Part of Jim's success has come through attracting experienced franchisees, some of whom have had experience with other chains, like Herman Li, and some, like Leighton Hull, who were already here when Jim arrived but have expanded their operations with Jim's assistance. (These are two franchisees whose stories you'll read about shortly.) Jim has also distributed information about Denny's in places where minority entrepreneurs might be looking; he hasn't just waited for prospective franchise owners to come to us. He has emphasized the availability of specific programs of financial aid for people interested in becoming franchisees. That financing is available to anyone, but it has proven especially helpful to minorities who may have difficulty in gaining access to capital. Most consistently, by just drilling it into his people that this work of adding to and diversifying the base of our franchises is important, he's managed to achieve very impressive results.

Restaurants: Easy to Eat in, Tough to Start up

Let's talk, for a second, about one of the toughest hurdles any minority entrepreneur faces when he or she wants to be a franchisee in a well-known chain: money. It isn't cheap these days to open a new restaurant. At Denny's what we often find is an entrepreneur, or entrepreneurial group, that has plenty of experience in the restaurant business but not enough money. Of course, sometimes we find the oppo-site—those individuals or groups with the money and not the experience, such as Akin Olajuwon, whom you'll hear more about. We have ways of helping people like that open restaurants, too. But often, it seems easier to work in a restaurant and learn the business than to come up with the financial wherewithal that owning a Denny's requires.

A prospective franchisee who wants to let us know he or she is serious about wanting to become part of Denny's can sign a development agreement for each restaurant to be developed. Not everyone has to pay this fee—only those who want to sign a development agreement for multiple restaurants in a specific geographic area. Then there is the franchise fee itself, which is $35,000. The development fee can be applied to that. After that, there is the cost of build-ing the restaurant itself, decorating it, and all the attendant costs. By the time the doors open, a franchisee has typically spent about $1.2 million for the new restaurant, though the figure may be less if an old building is remodeled than if a new one is built. Altogether, the franchisee will have to come up with, say, $250,000 in cash. And to make sure that we are dealing with serious, financially stable people—or groups—we also want them to have a net worth of about $750,000.

Coming up with this sort of cash is not always easy. So one of the tools that Jim has at his disposal is a program with the Finova Group, a financing company based in Scottsdale, Arizona, that helps out on the dollars and cents end. Since someone finances most of that $1.2 million for any prospective franchisee, what our program does is very simple. We help underwrite a percentage of the losses that the bank will take—and it will inevitably take some, as all lenders must. Since the bank knows that its risk is being cut on losses that it made on loans to entrepreneurs, it becomes a little more flexible in its standards and a little more willing to underwrite loans it might not otherwise consider.

Although this underwriting program is available to any potential franchisee at Denny's, it's especially helpful to prospective minority franchisees who tend to have more difficulty with financing than do our other partners. At the same time, it was an optional program, so that although it offered help, nobody who was African-American or Hispanic had to join in. It was not the only source for financing that we use, but it is one that we specifically developed for ourselves and that several of our minority-owned franchises have taken advantage of. Yes, they can use the Small Business Administration (SBA) or any other lender who will help them, but the fact is that for those on the border of what we consider financially acceptable, this program helps.

One of the other things we found as we tried to develop more minority franchises was how important it was to emphasize the nuts and bolts of simply getting a restaurant up and running. Again, like the loan program, this was help we offered to all franchisees, but help that many of our minority-franchisees found especially useful. That is doubly true for someone operating his or her first franchise. One of the other things we encourage these franchisees to do is to seek out a financial partner. If one person in the group has some background in the restaurant business and no cash, we encourage that person to consider bringing in a partner who may be interested in the franchise business and have the financial resources but not the experience.

We work with our franchisees as needed during the development stage and construction of their restaurants. We let them know what is required of them in terms of permit issues and the size of the building, for instance, and where and how to place the signs on their restaurants. We also advise them on staffing their restaurants—the size of the crew they will need and when they should start hiring and training them.

We might say, for instance, that once the franchisee has committed to a territory for his or her restaurant, it would make better sense to place it at site X rather than parcel Y because the traffic patterns at X are more favorable. (We do have final approval on the selection of a site.) We might follow up by saying that perhaps the franchisee should contact the owner of that particular piece of land or that building to initiate discussions.

At the next step, we might help with the permit process, which can be a nightmare for someone who has never built a commercial property before, and even go over the construction plans with the franchisee to ensure adherence to Denny's brand standards. We review them and make recommendations, but, as I say, they have to be recommendations. It's not hand-holding, but it is a process of making the whole enterprise a little easier for many of our franchisees who have never gone through the process before. The best reason to offer this support is so you won't have to do it again (you hope!) when the franchisee opens a second or third or fourth restaurant. Certainly, we believe in empowering all of our franchisees. In many circumstances, if franchisees can be successful at running a restaurant once, then they can be successful at it again. That, I think, is good for everybody.

I said before that there are people interested in the Denny's brand who want to run a restaurant and think they can make a good living at it but have no experience in the restaurant business. Working from such a position is not as foolish as it might seem. In addition, now that we have a good track record, it is easier and easier to attract potential applicants. In the last few years, many were deterred by our image problems. But with the care we've taken with these programs, we have a basis on which to persuade minority entrepreneurs to consider buying into Denny's, as opposed to McDonald's or KFC or any other chain you might care to name.

Money is certainly an important area for any franchisee. So is advice. But none of those things happened by accident. To get more minority franchisees here, one of the things Jim did was to make his staff think about the task in terms of everyday work. They had lots of goals and objectives to meet in that part of the business. Getting minority franchisees into the pipeline was one of those goals. It was an MBO—management by objective—aim on which all the managers had to focus as they went about their business.

Jim's staff is small but effective. In fact, a larger staff would probably have made achieving our goals more difficult. It was hard enough, with all the other things that the franchise group had to worry about, to keep track of how the group was handling its desire to expand the number of minority-owned franchises. It was a job that Jim's group carried out well because of the enormous managerial focus he put on it.

Working with Jim are three directors in charge of sales— the folks who actually try to get an applicant into the Denny's system. In addition, there are two real-estate specialists who help with the business of evaluating the right parcels of land on which the franchisee desires to build and three construction experts who review construction plans for the restaurants. They will answer questions, make referrals, and the like. All of these professionals are responsible for seeing that minority franchisees are included in the system.

Others in franchise development are, too. The sales force, for example, is one of the first contacts prospective franchisees make. They know that helping minority franchisees enter the system is an important part of their business. That was an emphasis that came from not just me or John or our board of directors but also from Jim, their immediate superior. Without his direction, this entire process, I think, would have been impossible. Before Jim came, there was a tendency for the sales force, for example, to be a lot of places, but not necessarily where the minority people were that we were counting on to come to Denny's. As I said earlier, we might advertise in *The Wall Street Journal* to find prospective owners, and yes, a lot of African-Americans read *The Wall Street Journal.* But those readers can be found in other places, too, so expanding our outreach was a big part of what's helped drive our numbers in this regard.

Another thing we've chosen to do is increase our presence at many of the trade shows and conferences frequented by black and other minority entrepreneurs. The Association of South East Asian Nations (ASEAN) conferences in California, for example, are gatherings where our salespeople can meet Asian entrepreneurs. The NAACP also has annual conventions where we can find people interested in becoming part of Denny's. Likewise, the La Raza conferences, held for Latinos, are a valuable source for connecting with minority entrepreneurs (Figure 9.1).

Figure 9.1   Denny's participates in several minority conferences and trade shows each year to attract potential minority franchise owners. This advertisement appeared in the 1998 annual conference program of the National Council of La Raza. Alfonso Fernandez owns three Denny's in Florida.

We've also expanded our search for franchise applicants to many more trade shows than we were doing just a few years ago. Because many prospective franchisees are motel and hotel operators who'd like to open a moderately priced restaurant within their site or nearby, we've started attending the national motel and hotel conventions. We also take in the Restaurant Leadership Conference, a trade show where companies that grant franchises and prospective franchisees meet. Similarly, because many truck stops on or near the interstates are also looking for round-the-clock restaurant operations, we have begun attending shows held by the National Association of Truck Stop Operators. If these operators are looking to brand their truck stops, we will happily become one of the brands that they are associated with. These are places we would not have been a few years ago, and yes, they are places where we find potential minority applicants as well as white ones.

Just because we wanted more minority owners as part of the business doesn't mean we'd lower our standards in any way or submit prospective minority franchisees to any less rigorous standards than any other group of restaurant operators. After all, we did not want another public-relations disaster like the Watts restaurant, which closed, in essence, because of a financially weak franchisee. Even for those who came financially prepared, we had to make sure they had the right qualities to be successful. This is not like another business. Remember, most Denny's are open 24 hours a day, every day. We have found instances in which some potential owners haven't quite thought through the implications of this. For example: You're the boss. It's two o'clock in the morning and your grill goes out. What happens? There is no one to call. You have to get out of bed, go to the restaurant, talk with the manager on duty, and try to solve the problem.

Typically, each Denny's has a general manager and two or three assistant managers. One of the assistant managers usually works the late-night shift. An established franchisee often hires someone for the general manager's slot as well as the assistants. But for a first-time franchisee, it isn't at all uncommon for the franchisee to be the general manager—which means he or she is the one to receive those late-night emergency calls. Can a person handle being in a business like this, being, in effect, on call all day and all night? And it isn't as if the managers are other family members, over whom the proprietor might wield familial influence when it comes to delegating some difficult or unpleasant duty.

In fact, we do not recommend having family members in the business. Most of our franchisees have found this wise advice and actually do not employ family members. But we do want to be sure our franchisees can handle the difficult and emergency situations that inevitably arise. Nevertheless, running a restaurant can still be an eye-opener for first-time franchisees, whether or not they are minorities, because they may be running a business for the first time. The dream of being a successful business owner may beckon, but the reality of running a business successfully may be altogether different.

Another thing that we look at is how well a person can really operate in a franchise system. The people who own these restaurants are buying a brand; like any brand-name product, it should be the same no matter where you partake of it. So we can't have people who are determined to be entrepreneurs but who will not do it within the parameters that Denny has set. We absolutely do not want to be seen as setting franchisees up for failure. It's a lot more fun to prime them to be successful franchisees—franchisees like Leighton Hull.

Leighton Hull, of Oxnard, California, came into our system in 1995; in that time, he has developed several Denny's franchises in California and is looking to expand. Leighton is not the kind of man who would be bothered with Denny's if he didn't think we were serious. "I've been a hard-core, card-carrying activist for many years," he said. "Denny's has made good on what they said they were going to do. The name of the game now is the board room, and if you don't change, you can't take advantages of the opportunities."

When It All Works, It Works Really Well

Leighton's activist credentials within the black community are notable. Not only has he been acquainted with some of the top leaders of the NAACP over the years, but he also was the economic coordinator for the Million Man March in Washington, D.C. in 1995. Leighton was an unhappy ex–franchise holder at McDonald's when he ended up applying to Denny's. Before that, he was a graduate of Indiana University who had also attended the entrepreneurial programs at Wharton and Harvard. He also worked for awhile as a marketing representative at Cummins Engine and at the Indiana Department of Commerce, helping minority businesses with technical assistance under a program sponsored by the federal government. Some of these things may not be what you'd expect a Harvard man to do, but Leighton, a native of South Bend, Indiana, knew what he wanted. "After leaving school, I decided to go back and give something to the community." It is not unusual for

African-Americans who have been fortunate in receiving a top-notch education to feel that they should use their skills and talents to benefit other black Americans who could use their help.

Leighton relocated to California in 1980 and did the same sort of business as a private consultant. That's when he got the franchise bug. He helped a client with an application to be a franchisee at Goodyear, the tire company. He spent weeks helping the client get the paperwork in order so that the bank would give the man the loan he needed to start the business. The bank approved the loan, and Goodyear was ecstatic at having gotten such an expertly prepared package. The company asked their new franchisee who had helped prepare his application. "Leighton Hull," the man said.

Goodyear got in touch and told Leighton how impressed they were with the documentation his client had presented. Would he be interested in running a Goodyear franchise himself, they wanted to know. Goodyear was so eager for Leighton to join them that they not only started looking for a site for his franchise but also pressed him to find other applicants. Leighton was ready to give it a try, and not just because he was an entrepreneur. It was 1984 and "My wife was going to have a child," Leighton said. "I needed a business that could go on without my actual presence all the time."

Now I would love to tell you that Leighton immediately picked up a phone and called Denny's—but that's not quite what happened. He decided to take a chance with what many outside the restaurant business consider the surest and safest of franchises: McDonald's. Said Leighton, "I had heard that McDonald's had tons of applications and it took years for them to approve you. I just put in there because I thought I had nothing to lose. I later heard that there were more than twenty-five thousand applications in 1984 and McDonald's acted on [only] two hundred twenty-five."

Leighton Hull's application was one of the 225. All McDonald's operators are expected to go to their headquarters for a period of training, and Leighton dutifully did his tenure at Hamburger University in suburban Chicago while his store was being constructed and his pregnant wife waited back home in metropolitan Los Angeles. He came back and his very own McDonald's was completed and opened in March 1985. In November of that year, his wife gave birth.

Leighton went on to build and open a second McDonald's franchise in southern California in 1989. As it is with most franchisees, it seemed easier the second time around. But it wasn't to stay that way. In the early 1990s, McDonald's, said Leighton, began to ratchet up the number of restaurants in the system. He says that some of those new restaurants opened up uncomfortably close to his franchises and ended up siphoning off customers that otherwise would have been his.

There was real friction between Leighton and McDonald's over this, and he ended up selling the two franchises back to McDonald's in 1995. Even before that happened, however, Leighton had taken a trip to Las Vegas, where he met up with an old friend—Fred Rasheed of the NAACP, who was negotiating the fair share agreement between the NAACP and Denny's. Rasheed said he was in Vegas for a business conference, and called Leighton, whose home was then in Pasadena. Over lunch in a casino hotel restaurant in Las Vegas, Rasheed broached the idea of a Denny's franchise to Leighton.

"He knew that they were interested in finding some minorities and African-Americans," said Leighton. "He also felt that Denny's was on the launch pad for growth and development as well as having signed on to the fair share projects. I told Fred I was interested in unlimited growth opportunities and I didn't care from whom."

To this day, Leighton maintains that the incidents that once plagued Denny's were the result not of systematic and planned discrimination but of the quality of some of the restaurants. "It does not," he said, "mean that you should condemn sixteen hundred other stores. At the time, I had heard about it, but I really didn't know a whole lot about what was going on. I figured nobody could be that stupid."

Leighton, as you can see, speaks his mind.

So he called up one of Denny's franchise representatives after meeting with Rasheed and had a frank discussion of the whole slew of incidents that had marred our reputation. Afterward, he was willing to enter into the process of becoming a franchisee with Denny's.

It takes roughly 90 days for an application to be approved. That's the time it takes for us to go over the paperwork and do our due diligence, for the applicant to come up with financing, and for us to make sure we have the right person. It takes roughly 9 months to 1 year after that for the restaurant to be constructed and the doors to open for business.

But within that time, we conduct a series of interviews to check on an applicant's integrity, reliability, and charac-ter—the things that count beyond financial assets. Every prospective franchisee has to come to Spartanburg and sit down for an interview with three people from headquarters. One is Jim Lyons, and the two others can vary—they can be from various divisions within the company, but one must always be a person of color. We want to show these potential franchisees that we are serious about diversity at the top levels, and we want to judge their seriousness about our goals at the same time.

This last phase of meeting with people from headquarters was not in place when I got here, though I did meet Leighton back in 1995, shortly after I arrived. The interview system, not fully operational until early 1998, was one of the innovations we have implemented over the past few years that is designed to strengthen our selection of franchisees. Those meetings, along with all the other actions I've described, have helped boost our numbers. Leighton, to this day, is cordial and enthusiastic about Denny's. Fred Rasheed, however, remembers nothing but footdragging surrounding Leighton's application to be a franchisee. Though Fred put in more than a good word, he thinks that some of the people in the system just took their sweet time about getting Leighton his approvals. Could be. But I know that that sort of thing could not happen now.

Leighton has come into our system with extraordinary energy. In 1995, he bought three of our company stores in Ventura County, California, and purchased three more Denny's stores in northern California in 1998. He built a new one last year in Ventura, California. All told, he now has seven franchises in the state and is currently working on acquiring more restaurants, including a new restaurant in Watts. With the funds from the sale of his McDonald's franchises, along with his prior experience of running a fran-

chise, Leighton certainly was ready to join the Denny's family (Figure 9.2).

On the other end of the spectrum, there are some people
who have access to capital but no experience. Akin
Olajuwon was one of those people. The brother of the
Houston Rockets basketball superstar, Hakeem Olajuwon,
he has loved eating at Denny's for many years, since he
went to college in Houston. He runs Olajuwon Holdings,
the company that eventually became a Denny's franchisee.
So why did he choose to invest in a Denny's franchise when
his only experience with the chain had been eating in its
restaurants? There is a theory on Wall Street that investors
do well by buying shares in the products they use themselves. I think something like this was operating for Akin.
He's said many times that in all the years he patronized
Denny's, nothing untoward ever happened to him. So no
one, he said, especially no one black, gives him any grief
about operating a string of Denny's restaurants.

I don't presume to speak for people of color, yet I think
Akin's experience points out the fact that our minority
franchisees can be a source of pride. We are getting the
word out that Denny's isn't the company it used to be. Said
Akin: "People actually support me because it is possible to
know that I haven't experienced any problems. I think it is
good for minorities to see that and for African-Americans
to know that."

When Akin decided in 1997 to become involved with
Denny's, we suggested that instead of building a new restaurant from scratch, Olajuwon Holdings buy some units from
the company instead. We wanted to see if he liked being in
the restaurant business and could do well at it, with the first
unit, a company-owned restaurant in Houston. The com-

LEIGHTON HULL, DENNY'S FRANCHISE OWNER

WE'RE CHANGING THE WAY YOU SEE DENNY'S.

A lot can change in a few years. Take a look at what's happening at Denny's. By the end of 1996, the number of minority-owned Denny's franchises had grown to 160. And by the end of 1997, there will be many more.

And that's not all. In 1996, Denny's contracted 80 million dollars in business to minority suppliers, and was once again the largest corporate contributor to the Save the Children STAR (Serious Teens Acting Responsibly) program, created to empower at-risk youth.

At Denny's, we believe everyone deserves a healthy piece of the pie. Creating and sharing that vision are what we're all about. So, when you look at Denny's, you can see an opportunity for the American dream to come true.

DENNY'S. A TOTAL COMMITMENT TO A NEW ERA.

© 1997 DFO, Inc.

Figure 9.2   Leighton Hull is one of Denny's over 100 minority franchise owners. A Denny's franchisee since 1995, Hull now owns seven Denny's in California and is looking to expand. He was featured in a Denny's print advertisement that appeared in *Black Enterprise Magazine, Jet,* and *Ebony.*

pany was wildly successful with that unit and Olajuwon Holdings proceeded to build 4 more units around the city— and then to venture out even farther, buying 10 more units from the company in metropolitan Detroit.

Of course the deal that put Olajuwon Holdings in the news came in March 1998, when it purchased 63 restaurants from another Denny's franchisee, Phoenix Restaurant Group, Inc. (formerly DenAmerica), for $28.7 million. (Olajuwon Holdings financed the acquisition through a division of Deutsche Bank, one of the largest financial institutions in the world.) Some of these restaurants were also in Texas, with others scattered throughout 12 eastern states. The restaurants, said Phoenix Restaurant Group at the time, were sold to reduce corporate debt. The deal made Olajuwon Holdings not only the largest minority franchisee of Denny's but also the second largest Denny's franchisee (Figure 9.3).

People often ask me when Denny's will expand into some areas of the country where we currently don't have a large presence. Why aren't we in the central-city areas of New York or Washington or Philadelphia, or in other parts of the Northeast where we are currently underrepresented? Well, we won't stay out of those communities forever. Big cities are certainly more expensive to operate in than are many of the suburban and smaller communities in the Southwest or California where Denny's has traditionally had its strongest presence. Still, in the not-too-distant future, we plan to move up the northeast corridor.

In fact, we plan to open up one or two Denny's Classic Diners in Connecticut, all around the city of New Haven. They will be owned by one of our Asian-American franchisees, Herman Li. The Denny's diners are a new twist on

Golden West Foods Corporation
Leighton Hull
Denny's multi-unit franchisee

"Denny's greatest strength lies within its invisible assets. These assets are not reflected on the financial balance sheet, but include consumer trust, brand image, corporate culture, creativity, competitiveness, experience, management savvy and franchisor/franchisee joint competitive focus. Franchisor/franchisee cooperation is a competitive advantage that increases brand value. The results are obvious. With franchisee input, Denny's has repositioned itself as America's number one 'diner'. It's a good time to be a part of Denny's."

QK, Inc.
Robbie Qualls & Doug Koch
Denny's multi-unit franchisee

"We started out washing dishes at Denny's years ago and worked for the company as franchise representatives until we bought our first restaurant. We grew up in the Denny's corporate system and became franchisees in 1990. We haven't found any other concept that offers the return on investment and fits into so many versatile areas."

BR Associates, Inc.
Robert Ruckriegel
Denny's multi-unit and multi-concept franchisee

"Our theory has always been you will never replace the good old coffee shop that serves a great cup of coffee and a diverse menu of great meals for all three dayparts and a late night snack. Denny's is the largest there is with the opportunity to grow 1,000 units much stronger and faster than anyone else. At Denny's, you can give guests more personal service by serving their coffee at their table with a friendly smile."

Olajuwon Holdings, Inc.
Akinola Olajuwon, President
Denny's multi-unit franchisee

"As a strong family business, we are pleased to be associated with the Denny's brand, which is the leader among family-style restaurants. My association with Denny's began as a customer during my college days in Houston, where Denny's always offered outstanding food and good service at reasonable prices."

Figure 9.3 Denny's franchising packet features statements from several multi-unit franchise owners including Akin Olajuwon of Olajuwon Holdings, Inc., the second largest franchisee in the Denny's system, which owns over 75 restaurants in several states. This is a page from the franchising packet, which is distributed to prospective franchisees.

our traditional restaurants that we expect will do well for us, with a slightly expanded menu and a totally different look. The restaurants are shinier, with more chrome than our traditional places. They're a touch retro in appearance while being thoroughly up-to-date in terms of systems and menus. They really do remind you of an old-fashioned diner. They've already tested well, and we plan to open many of them in the coming years.

Herman is an experienced franchiseholder who also happens to be familiar with many of our managers here at Advantica because of his franchise history with Burger King. He started with Burger King in 1979, when he opened up his first franchise in Redondo Beach, California. I'd like to say that Herman was attracted to Burger King when I was there because of something I'd done, but I'd be kidding you if I said that. Herman, then an eager and entrepreneurial-minded 25-year-old tired of the corporate grind, came to Burger King because he had made no progress, he says, in his efforts to land a franchise at McDonald's.

Well, Herman no longer owns that Redondo Beach Burger King, but he has managed to become one of the top 10 Burger King franchise owners. His C&L Restaurants, based in Los Angeles, owns 80 restaurants across seven states.

Although Herman is based in Los Angeles, his franchises span the country. But, until recently at least, they were all Burger King franchises. Herman says that in 1998, C&L felt the need to diversify its portfolio. So how did he come our way? "The Burger King network is still very strong," he says. That's an understatement, I guess! Herman has kept in touch with various members of Advantica's management team, occasionally talking to John Romandetti, Ray Hood-Phillips, or me, even after we all left Miami.

It was at the 1998 Restaurant Leadership Conference in Monterey, California, a trade show for Asian entrepreneurs, that Herman bumped into Jim Lyons again. They spent time chatting, and Herman became intrigued with the idea of becoming a Denny's franchisee. He sits on the board of the Diversity Action Committee at Burger King, a group that exists to further minority participation at all levels at that company. He is also involved with the Asian-American business community in many different organizations, and as a part of that wider community, he invited Denny's and Advantica to an Asian-America trade show in California later on, where he and members of Jim's sales staff continued to explore the idea of Herman's adding to his franchise portfolio by becoming a Denny's franchisee.

By the end of the year, Herman's group had purchased the three Denny's restaurants in Connecticut, where it already had some of its Burger King franchises, and was beginning the process of turning them into Denny's diners in 1999 and 2000. Herman also has a development agreement with Denny's to bring eight more restaurants to the state over the next three years. Not only does Herman believe that the Denny's diner concept is a winner but he also understands and believes in the philosophy by which we run the company, that diversity is in and of itself a good thing, and that it is also good for business. We're glad he has decided to work with us and glad he is helping to bring the newest phase of Denny's to the northeast, where we have traditionally been underrepresented.

No matter where our restaurants are, though, we're always looking for the right people to own them. Even though every franchisee and company-owned restaurant has to make an attempt to be a good neighbor by getting involved in the community, those efforts need to be especially prominent in minority neighborhoods. The restaurant can't just open the doors, rake in the money, and expect to thrive without active participation with its neighbors. I think that someone reading this may be willing to take Denny's to the next level, doing good in the community as well as doing well financially. Are you entrepreneurial and willing to take the risk and earn the rewards? Call Jim Lyons. He'd love to hear from you.

CHAPTER

10

New People, New Directions

I have dinner with 10 extraordinary men and women who gather in New York or California five or six times a year to manage a project close to my heart: Advantica. These people are our directors. Every year, Advantica pays them each $30,000, in addition to some stock and stock options, to come together and provide the company with oversight and direction. We meet for dinner the night before the formal board meetings to informally discuss business and to reacquaint ourselves with each other. One of the things I'm proudest of, of course, is that we have a diverse group of board members, men and women who literally embody our values.

Looking out at our board members who sat in the front row of the audience during our annual meeting at the Waldorf Astoria in May 1999, I couldn't help but be grateful to and proud of these people. I also couldn't help noticing that it was a very different group of people than the directors I started working with when I came to Advantica in 1995. Through a bankruptcy and the subsequent reorganization of the company, an awful lot of the faces on that board have changed—most of them, in fact. But one thing that has not changed since I joined the company is its commitment to diversity and inclusion, a commitment that extends into the boardroom. If anything, that commitment has grown. With 2 African-American directors on our board, I believe we have more representation by people of color on our board of directors now than do most companies with boards of a similar size. For all practical purposes, there are 2 additional persons of color on our board, 1 African-American and 1 Latino. Technically, they are on the board of directors of FRD Acquisition, an Advantica subsidiary that oversees our Coco's and Carrows restaurants. You won't see them listed in Advantica's filings with the Securities and Exchange Commission, for instance. But they participate in our board meetings. They're pictured in our 1998 annual report along with Advantica's directors because they attend Advantica board meetings and contribute to meetings as Advantica directors do. Their inclusion makes our board of directors one of the most diverse, I believe, of any large company board in the country. Our de facto board of directors, then, has 11 members, 3 of them African-American and 1 Latino. I don't think you will find too many boards at big companies with 36% of their directors being people of color.

Before I tell you how we made this change, let me introduce you to our directors:

- Ronald Blaylock runs one of the largest and most prestigious minority-owned investment houses in the country. In 1999, he achieved some notice when he managed to become an underwriter in the largest bond offering ever, the sale of $6 billion of bonds for AT&T.

- Dr. Vera King Farris was the first African-American member on Advantica's board of directors. She is an educator and president of Richard Stockton College of New Jersey, a liberal arts college in Pomona.

- James Gaffney is chairman of Vermont Investments Ltd., a holding company with diverse manufacturing and distribution interests. He also has years of experience as CEO of various businesses, including apparel, home furnishings, toys, and giftware, as well as swimming-pool equipment and construction.

- Irwin Gold is a senior managing director of Houlihan, Lokey, Howard, and Zukin, a Los Angeles–based investment banking firm that serves midmarket companies.

- Darrell Jackson is a South Carolina state senator and an ordained minister. He is an entrepreneur as well, serving as president of a marketing and consulting firm, Sunrise Enterprise of Columbia, South Carolina.

- Robert Marks is the president of Marks Ventures Inc., a venture capital fund. He was formerly with Carl Marks & Co.

- Charles Moran is retired from Sears Roebuck & Co., where he was the chief administrative officer.

- Elizabeth Sanders, one of two female board members, is a management consultant and a former vice president at Nordstrom, Inc. She is the author of the best-selling book *Fabled Service: Ordinary Acts, Extraordinary Outcomes*, based on her years with the retailer.

- Donald Shepherd is the retired chairman of Loomis, Sayles, & Co., an investment firm based in Boston, Massachusetts. Loomis, Sayles is Advantica's largest shareholder with about 22% of the company's common shares.

- Raul Tapia is a lawyer and senior partner at Murray, Scheer, Montgomery, Tapia, & O'Donnell, a government relations consulting firm with offices in Washington, D.C., London, and Moscow. He is also extremely active in HACR, the Hispanic Association on Corporate Responsibility, of which Advantica is a corporate member. He is also chairman of the Hispanic Heritage Awards Foundation.

Some Tough Questions

Assembling this group was, of course, no accident. It took work, and some of that work started before I got here. My predecessor, Jerry Richardson, who had signed the fair share agreement with the NAACP, was responsible for recruiting the first African-American member of the board, Dr. Vera King Farris. When the company, then Flagstar, agreed to sign the moral covenant that was the fair share agreement with the NAACP, its board of directors had no African-Americans. There was, however, one Hispanic-Asian member of the board, Michael Chu, who was then a senior officer of KKR, the firm that saved TW by investing in it. Vera knew of the difficulties at Flagstar, but she admits that she was a little shocked when she got the call in the summer of 1993.

"Spencer Stuart [an executive search firm that the company used] gave me call in August or September to see whether I would be interested," says Vera. "They told me that they were interviewing a number of other people, but I was notified in late November that my name had gone forward." Vera is an engaging and energetic woman, an educator of long standing who often shows up at board meetings with a wide smile and any one of several wonderfully evocative hats. If she was going to come onto the board, she would, in her own words, "interview them while they were interviewing me."

So in the fall, Vera came to New York for lunch in the dining room at the offices of KKR (Kohlberg Kravis Roberts & Co.) on West 57th Street, just off of Fifth Avenue. Meeting there made sense, of course, because the firm had recently invested $300 million in Flagstar's future. That money would keep the company from going under for a while but would not ultimately be enough to overcome all its problems. But for a while, at least, that investment also made KKR the majority owner, giving it enough seats to control the board. One of those seats belonged to Paul Raether, the KKR partner who lured me to the company from Burger King and with whom I am still friends today —even though KKR lost its investment in the company. Another seat belonged to Henry Kravis, one of the name partners of KKR. Three other KKR executives, Clifton Robbins, Mike Tokarz, and George Roberts, also were installed on the board as part of the deal that let Jerry Richardson and the company have the $300 million. A fourth seat belonged to Michael Chu, a former KKR executive who is now president and chief executive officer of ACCION International, a nonprofit organization that makes microloans in poor communities around the world. That gave KKR six of the nine seats on the board, guaranteeing its decision-making power.

That's one reason that Paul Raether will say, even today, that board meetings throughout 1994 and into 1995, until Richardson left the company, were relatively calm, despite the two big problems going on at Flagstar at the time: sales were dropping at Hardee's, and Denny's was facing mounting nationwide criticism because of the discrimination suits. Still, Vera was not going to join this club without checking it out a little more closely. She certainly did not see herself becoming the first black person on the board of a company as notorious as the one that owned Denny's, just to let it save face. If she was going to start making trips to Spartanburg, South Carolina, with any regularity, and have to explain to her friends and family why she was going, she wanted to be sure she was right.

Vera was intensely aware that one of the reasons she was being wooed for the board was because she was black. At the same time, she didn't want that to be the only reason she was being considered. So in November of 1993 she talked with Paul and Jerry for hours, over lunch, about how the debt situation would affect the company. She was concerned about the enormous debt—about $2.2 billion at that time—that hung over the company's head and whether the financing provided by KKR, which had cut some of the company's financing costs, would be enough to save it. Vera, after all, was running a large organization herself. Worries about budgets and cash flow and dealing with financial projections were not unknown to her.

Anyhow, she had made up her mind, even before going in to KKR's offices, that she did not want to be talked to crudely about race, or even solely about race, though she was sure the topic would come up. "I spent a good deal of time talking about the role of a director," says Vera. "I had to be cognizant of the role of the shareholders; that's primary. But I could not ignore the fact that I am a minority. It was a sensitive situation. If any of them had just come out and said directly, 'What should we do about our problems? You're black; you should know,' I would have walked out the door right then and there."

So Vera, Paul, and Jerry took their time getting to know each other, testing the waters. "I had to decide whether this was an area in which I would spend my time," says Vera, who had her hands full working to educate the 6,100 students at Richard Stockton; those students were her primary responsibility. "My first reaction was that I had spent a goodly part of my life attempting to bring together groups, so I saw this as an enormously intriguing challenge." Vera had spent many years as an educator bridging the racial divides that pop up on campus and in the academic world in which she participated.

Still, despite the obvious negative possibilities, Vera was warming to the challenge of helping our company find its way to fiscal and social health. "The company's heavy debt burden did come up, and my concern was that with the heavy burden of the lawsuits, too, where were they going to go? But that did not interest me as much as whether a major corporation could change its racism and be a force for diversity."

Vera will now be the first to tell you that a company can indeed make that change. By May 1994, she was sitting with the directors during the annual meeting. She believes so strongly in what we have done that she has become one of the most vocal and public supporters of Denny's and Advantica that we could ever hope to have. Recently, I have cut back on speaking engagements about the challenges of inclusivity at Denny's and how we addressed them to focus on Advantica business overall; it takes up less and less of my time. But not so with Vera. The more successful we become at making ourselves the inclusive and diverse company we aspire to be, the more she's willing to tell other people about it.

Don't let her be in attendance at any gathering at which someone begins to bash Denny's without the facts! She'll be the first on her feet to, shall we say, correct, the lady or gentleman with the erroneous information. At the annual meeting of the American Council of Education in February 1999, for instance, Vera wandered into a room where a panel discussion was going on, and a member of the panel was talking about how woeful Denny's was in terms of what it had accomplished. Vera says now that she took the time to correct the gentleman—publicly—about the matter in question. "I don't even remember what it was now," she says, "but I absolutely refuse to have people say something wrong about Denny's."

Our board really did work smoothly, in large part because of the preponderance of KKR people running the show. Shortly after they took control of the situation, Paul and the rest of the KKR contingent on the board mentioned to Jerry that it was time for the company to increase the number of minorities in the upper ranks of the company. Jerry was not at all opposed to this in the year before I arrived at the company. Both Paul and Vera also say one of the reasons the board had no problems coming to terms with the claims of discriminatory treatment it faced was because of Jerry's essentially nonprejudiced nature. He just was not by any means a mean guy. "He was a person of high energy and sincere commitment to the food service business, and he was a self-made man, too. He was shocked the appellation *racist* would be applied to him," says Vera. "I even visited him at home many times, and he was not racist with me."

I think her radar is very good and, for the most part, correct. Jerry was never the embodiment of corporate racism that he's so often made out to be. He certainly would not have been that way at a lunch where he tried to woo Vera onto the board. But she maintains to this day that if he had any hidden "dark side," she would have seen it at least once after she joined the board in late 1993 and before he left it in 1995.

We have a less complex organization right now, with only our four core businesses, Denny's, Coco's, Carrows, and El Pollo Loco—and we expect to sell El Pollo Loco. But back then there were a lot more units, and Vera's take on it was that the organization had grown so large that Jerry could not effectively monitor everything that was happening in it. In 1993, we still had our Hardee's franchises, we still had Quincy's, the steakhouse chain, and El Pollo Loco had not yet been put on the block. "The organization had grown so large by then, but Richardson assumed that his own personal philosophy was pervasive everywhere," Vera said. "From the day he started, he was on top of everything." But the size of the organization precluded that now. It was no longer possible for every franchise and restaurant to reflect the character of the boss, she felt. Still, she came away from that long lunch with Paul and Jerry impressed. "I had," she says, "the deep sense that they were sincere and we talked at that interview about knowing the future as well as dwelling in the past."

Because the board had so many people from KKR, they could do what they thought best for the shareholders—and

KKR was the biggest shareholder at the time—with no serious opposition. That still didn't make some of the actions it decided to take any easier. The board decided it needed fresh leadership if Flagstar was going to move to the next level. Jerry Richardson was pursuing his dream of owning an NFL franchise, which would bring big-time sports to Charlotte, North Carolina, so he had the Carolina Panthers as a new and exciting opportunity to pursue when he left Flagstar.

When I finally did decide to come to Spartanburg, my presence at the board meetings of Flagstar was actually rather anticlimactic. Since the board wooed me, and most of the board came from the same company—KKR—it wasn't as if I had to rally the directors to my side. They were on my side from the start. And although any chief executive takes the time to meet his board, they were much more interested in my turning the company around than in my giving any dramatic speech and pounding my fists on the table, screaming about how we had to make some changes around here. Well, clearly we did. But since the board already knew that—it is why they hired me—from the first, our meetings were cordial and low key. I don't think any of the directors expected any more from me than that, even at the start. As Paul Raether puts it, "It was a board that functioned perfectly normally."

Two members of the board told Jerry in September 1994 that his tenure would end the following year. The bad news was delivered to him at KKR's offices in New York City, where he had gone to take care of some matter now long forgotten. "It's never easy to go and tell somebody like Jerry, who has a substantial portion of his life tied up in his job, something like this," said Paul Raether. "When we [he and Mike Tokarz] told him that maybe it was time to move on, Jerry said to me, 'I never thought I'd be told to get another job.' I told him that he didn't need another job; he already had one where he spent a lot of time—football. The Carolina Panthers." I think it's a tribute to Jerry, to KKR, and to Flagstar's board of directors that the transition from his leadership to mine went as smoothly as it did.

A New Set of Problems—and a New Set of Opportunities

Of course all of us at Flagstar worked hard from 1995, when I arrived, until early 1997, trying to right the increasingly tenuous financial position of the company—too much debt and not enough cash to service it. We couldn't do it. When we decided near the end of 1996 that the company would have to go through a financial reorganization in early 1997, it meant an excruciating round of late-night, last-minute negotiations with our creditors. Because the bankruptcy meant that the shares of common stock owned by our major investor, KKR, basically become worthless, the KKR managers would no longer be represented on the board after Flagstar's bankruptcy was discharged. The company would start off with a new name—Advantica—and a new board as well, one that would be selected largely by the former Flagstar bondholders who gave up their Flagstar bonds to become Advantica shareholders.

It was clear to me that even though the bankruptcy and restructuring would put the company on a stronger financial footing, we'd still have to deal with making Advantica a fully inclusive and diverse workplace, especially at the highest levels—meaning the board of directors. So I set out to see how to maneuver additional people of color onto the board of the new company, Advantica.

In a bankruptcy, the existing shares of a company become essentially worthless—personally, I lost the thousands of shares of Flagstar stock that I owned when we entered Chapter 11—and the bondholders are the creditors that have to be satisfied first. Since one of the things that satisfies them is equity ownership in the company that emerged from Chapter 11, that meant that they also had a substantial say in who the directors of Advantica would be. In fact, in the agreement that brought Flagstar out of bankruptcy, I was allowed to remain chairman of the board and was also given the right to name two other members to the new Advantica board of directors. In addition, I spoke with the representative of large bondholders who were becoming stockholders. One of the largest of this group was Moore Capital Management, which is based in Rockefeller Center in New York City. Moore is currently a shareholder that emerged from the bankruptcy with just fewer than 10% of the common stock of Advantica.

I convinced Moore to select a minority member for Advantica's new board. The people at Moore, though, already had a candidate in mind, so I didn't have to suggest one. One of the former principals there, George Haywood, suggested Ron Blaylock, an energetic young African-American, who, only in his late thirties, was already running his own investment house, with about 50 employees. Ron is a former basketball player at Georgetown University. After graduating from Georgetown, on the same Hoyas team that included New York Knicks superstar Patrick Ewing, Ron headed to Wall Street. He's a smart guy. Not only was he a top notch ballplayer—better than I ever was—but he also managed to set the course for his future when he was in college by spending a summer interning at A. G. Becker on its trading floor. Later, he was 1 of only 2 undergraduates among the 24 candidates—the rest had master of business administration degrees—to be accepted at Citicorp's investment bank capital markets training program. Ron worked there, at PaineWebber, and at another black-owned securities firm, Utendahl Capital Partners, before starting his own shop with some financial backing from Bear Stearns. That company, it has been reported, put $10 million into Ron's new firm in exchange for a 25% stake in it.

Like Vera King Farris before she joined the board, Ron Blaylock knew of the company mostly from the newspaper headlines and television news reports, not firsthand. So he, too, was not sure he ought to sit on the board of the company that owned the infamous Denny's. But as chief executive officer, I was the one to talk with him, explain who we really were and what we were doing, and address any other concerns he might have about Denny's and Advantica. Sometime in the middle of 1997, when it actually looked like we could see an end to the bankruptcy, I flew up to Ron's offices in New York City. Investment bankers, in case you haven't met any recently, really do tend to be conservative dressers—wing tips, suspenders, French cuffs, and the like. Me, I'm more casual. When I met with Ron at his office in New York, I dressed in my usual attire, a shirt and tie, but also jeans and a blazer. I gave him my speech about why he should join us at Advantica and take one of the seats on the board of directors. He was very cool. But he decided to take a few days and think about it anyway. He took the weekend to mull it over, perhaps talk with some of his friends and colleagues, and called me the Monday afterward to accept. Like almost anyone who has come to work at Advantica in the past few years, and especially anyone black, you have to be convinced that Denny's is sincere in its desire to build a more equitable workplace.

What I said must have worked. Ron Blaylock is now on our board of directors. And after a few years with Advantica, I'm confident that he understands the core beliefs about fairness, diversity, and inclusion that are fundamental to Denny's and to all of Advantica. In addition to that, he can contribute his super financial expertise immediately. Ron's company's expertise is in raising funds. It has become one of the best-known black investment houses in the country, raising funds for everyone from the Tennessee Valley Authority to AT&T.

On the new Advantica board, I was given the right, under the agreement that came out of the restructuring, to appoint two people. Since Vera had preceded this restructuring, and indeed, had preceded me at the company, it was pretty easy to renominate her. My second choice was not a minority but another woman who had joined Flagstar's board in 1995—Elizabeth Sanders. She runs her own consulting firm and also is an experienced board member, having served as a director at Wal-Mart, H. F. Ahmanson, and Wolverine Worldwide, among other firms.

One of the things that I want to say is that every member of our board is also attuned to Advantica's finances. That means we're all reading from the same book when it comes to getting the company out of the red and making it one of the most profitable restaurant companies in the United States. We are not there yet, but I like to believe that we are getting close with every passing month. You'd have expected that back when KKR ruled the roost here. Henry Kravis, Mike Tokarz, and all the rest of the KKR contingent were forthcoming about all the problems the company faced and backed me fully in my efforts to resolve them. What you may find just as surprising is that the same unity of purpose exists now at Advantica's board of directors. We aren't generally a warm and fuzzy bunch; we don't do any of the trendy things some corporate boards do to "bond," such as going on canoe trips or taking Outward Bound courses. Anyway, most of our members are far too busy for that. They fly in, meet at dinner the night before, and go on to the board meeting the next day. So we do what we need to do and then go home to our businesses and our families.

And who are the two board members who are part of our FRD subsidiary, the wholly owned arm of Advantica that runs Coco's and Carrows? Well, one got there by my getting my ear chewed off by Rick Bela, who is a past president of HACR, the Hispanic Association on Corporate Responsibility. About 32% of our employees are Hispanic, and we already signed an agreement with HACR shortly after I arrived to enhance economic opportunities for this important segment. That agreement also sought to increase the number of Hispanic franchise owners, suppliers, and management. So when Rick heard that the reconstituted board at Advantica would not have any Hispanic members on it, he gave me hell over the phone. And, like a parent who has just the right touch, he added, "Jim, I'm disappointed in you." That did it. Though we mean to be an inclusive company, we aren't going to be able to have a representative of every ethnic group in America on our board. But with the Hispanic population growing so quickly, and in many of the markets that are most important to us, such as California, it was a situation I wanted to rectify as quickly as possible.

I had already filled the two slots on the board that were awarded to the CEO after the restructuring. So increasing the minority representation would take a bit of corporate maneuvering, a task I managed to accomplish in 1998. Our Coco's and Carrows subsidiaries have always been set up under a completely different subsidiary than the other lines of business here, Denny's and El Pollo Loco. That subsidiary's board had two vacancies on it. And although I was limited in the number of directors I could appoint to Advantica, because the FRD subsidiary had never been in the bankruptcy—only Flagstar, the corporate umbrella, was involved—I was free to fill those posts as I wanted, and to go beyond that, making the people I chose de facto members of the Advantica board who sit in, discuss ideas and strategies, and contribute what they can to the board meetings. But they do not vote on any Advantica matters.

So the two people I chose for the FRD board were Raul Tapia and Darrell Jackson. Unlike the wooing I had to do to attract Vera and Ron to the board, these were individuals with prior contact with the company. So they knew who we really were. There was no deep soul-searching on the same level that accompanied our bids to get Vera and Ron to sit on the board. Raul, because he had HACR in common with Advantica, knew us and was glad to join us. Rick Bela recommended him because he knows his way around the nation's capital. Raul is a long-time Washington insider. Every board member is chosen because he or she contributes something to the corporation. Both his inside-the-Beltway knowledge and his ability to help us better understand our

Spanish-speaking customers are big reasons that Raul is a member of the board.

Sometimes you also need people who can contribute to your board by telling you what is going on locally, or at the state level. Of course Advantica is located in South Carolina and we all read the newspapers and watch the television news. But it never hurts to have a board member who is more knowledgeable about state and local politics and who knows what is going on at the grassroots level. For us, that was Darrell Jackson. As if he isn't already busy enough, what with being a state senator here in South Carolina and a minister, too, he had already known about Advantica and its businesses in many of its previous incarnations, going back to the TW days.

All of us on the board are in this together. Being black or speaking Spanish or being a woman, in and of itself, is not enough to help this company do what it needs to do. Once, some years after Vera King Farris was on the board and when the company still owned its Hardee's units, she traveled south from New Jersey to visit the Hardee's test kitchens in South Carolina. Senator Jackson was showing her around. "From the time I was named to the board, I went down to Spartanburg to find out what was really going on. At the time, I spent a lot of time touring tasting kitchens and biscuit bakeoffs. You know, they offered to show me how to make a really good biscuit, but I declined," says Vera, who toured the kitchens with the senator. "I didn't want anyone to think I could actually cook!" Well, our board is smart, versatile, diverse, and collegial. But please, if you ever see Vera, don't ask her for a recipe for biscuits. Right now all my directors are happy. I'd like to keep it that way!

11

Celebrating Success

Dressed in an elegant black pantsuit, Ray Hood-Phillips took the stage at the Advantica auditorium. It was early morning, yet the atmosphere was one more akin to a festive awards night. In fact, Ray was the mistress of ceremonies for the only public acknowledgment of excellence supported by the company. The occasion was the second annual Abrazo awards, and its purpose was simple—to honor those 10 men and women who had done the most in the previous year to foster and advance the mission of a diverse and inclusive workplace at Advantica.

This awards ceremony is so special to me. It's such a privilege to work with people like the ones we honor here; it makes me proud to lead a company that could bring such people together. Part cheerleader, part missionary, Ray welcomed the employees who had taken their places in the 200-seat auditorium and reminded them of why they had gathered.

"*Abrazo* means 'to embrace' in Spanish. We're here today to honor the ten individuals who really embrace the concept of inclusiveness and diversity.

"1998 was a wonderful year for Advantica in terms of diversity. I did not think we could top the 60 *Minutes* story about Denny's that ran in the spring. It was a very, very positive story that told what happened behind the scenes at Denny's, [which] I'm sure just shocked America, because they had been hearing all these other things.

"So imagine our surprise when *Fortune* magazine ranked Advantica number two in the country. Some of you may not know that they surveyed twelve hundred companies and they picked the top fifty in the nation and we ranked number two."

The sound of applause filled the packed auditorium. The gathered employees had, for several years now, felt the sting of embarrassment about where they worked, worrying about whether they, too, would be perceived as part of the way their company had been perceived—a hotbed of racism and backward employment practices. Now, after a long siege, there was reason to celebrate (Figure 11.1).

When the applause faded, Ray went on to talk about her first major meeting with employees at Advantica, in the spring of 1995. It was at a support center meeting, a quarterly meeting for headquarters employees held in the same auditorium. I had asked Ray to speak to employees about the vision and the mission for the newly created Diversity Affairs Department.

"I began thinking and dreaming. And I said, 'You know what I really want? I really want to take this unfortunate place where we are right now and turn it inside out and right-side up, so that we would become a model for the restaurant industry—no! for all of corporate America—a model of how

Figure 11.1   John Romandetti, president and chief executive officer of Denny's, and Ray Hood-Phillips, chief diversity officer for Advantica, celebrate the company's success in changing the culture to one that embraces diversity. (Photo courtesy of the *Charlotte Observer*.)

a company manages diversity to the company's benefit of the bottom line, to really leverage it in the marketplace.'"

"And as I was preparing for today, I thought, 'Wow, we did it!' Because not a day goes by that Jim, John Romandetti, or [I] don't get calls from companies. These companies are not only inside our industry but also outside our industry. Now other organizations call; colleges and universities [and] churches call. They ask, 'How did you do it? What's your plan? What's your model? What's your secret?' So miracles can happen. They can—when you believe in the mission, when you believe in the vision and the team.'"

As her opening remarks concluded, Ray explained how the 10 honorees were chosen. Each member of the 10-member senior management team searches his or her group, for the man or woman who has done the most in the previous year to further the cause of diversity and inclusion at Advantica. At the awards ceremony, the senior management leader of each area introduces the team member receiving the awards, explains the person's contribution to the company's diversity progress, and presents the person with a gold Advantica Abrazo Achiever lapel pin and a small gift in honor of the day.

I presented the first of the 10 awards. "I'm glad to have a chance to recognize a member of the senior leadership team who's made a difference at Advantica, and at the company he runs," I began. "My choice this year is Nelson Marchioli, president of El Pollo Loco. I gave Nelson a very difficult assignment this year. Frankly I wanted to see more women and minorities in management at the company, but I also wanted to see more [white people] at El Pollo Loco. At the end of this year, he achieved exactly what I asked. His workforce statistics now closely mirror the demographics for the communities they serve.

"He managed to bring a more balanced representation of whites, minorities, and women to the company. He decreased the high minority percentage from sixty-seven percent to sixty percent and increased female representation in management from zero to thirty percent. The El Pollo Loco officer group remained twenty-five percent minority, while minority directors went from zero percent to forty-four percent. These are important shifts that make the company more reflective of the marketplace."

Nelson joined me on stage to receive his award as his name flashed on the large screen behind him. Dressed in a gray suit and tie, his angular face looking boyish as he stepped to the podium, Nelson related the story of his surprise at being chosen. "I called Ray about a month and a half ago and said I think someone made a mistake. I got e-mail about being a recipient of the Abrazo award, and I think you meant to send it to Eric Ewers. And Ray left me a voicemail that said, 'No, it's *you*.'

"Jim Adamson creates a working environment that allows us to do the right thing," he added, in his thanks to the many team members who work in concert with him at El Pollo Loco. "We do the right thing at E1 Pollo Loco because we hire the right people."

The entire morning was devoted to the recognition of people like Nelson Marchioli. John Romandetti of Denny's presented an award to Susan Schneider, director of special promotions and community relations, for her work in creating partnerships with groups such as the Harlem Globetrotters and the Hispanic Heritage Awards Foundation; in creating a Black History Month teaching curriculum; and in her oversight of Denny's partnership with Save the Children. Save the Children receives almost $1 million a year from Denny's, its largest corporate sponsor (Figure 11.2).

Craig Bushey, the president of Carrows and Coco's, presented an award to Tony Falls, director for international operations and training. Tony is responsible for the 300-plus Coco's restaurants in Japan, Korea, the United Arab Emirates, and China.

Nelson Marchioli of E1 Pollo Loco returned to the stage to present an Abrazo award to Eric Ewers, an area leader at the company. Eric received the award for his work in recruiting African-Americans to the ranks of management at the West Coast chain, whose work force is largely Hispanic. The number of African-Americans on Eric's management team grew from 8% to 21% in a single year.

Rhonda Parish, Advantica's general counsel, presented the award for her division to Rob Barrett, assistant general

We don't just feed the body,

we feed the Spirit.

Our kids. After school, they need caring adults. Safe places. Constructive activities. The very things Save the Children is providing through its Web of Support for U.S. children. That's why Denny's is the largest corporate sponsor of Save the Children. It's part of our continuing commitment to nurture the next generation.

Denny's is committed to providing the best possible service to all customers, regardless of race, creed, color or national origin.

©1999 DFO, Inc.

Figure 11.2   Denny's has contributed more than four million dollars to support Save the Children initiatives that primarily serve minority children in the United States.

counsel whom you read about earlier, for his tireless work as the lead counsel with oversight of the two consent decrees, as well as his work with the Department of Justice and the Office of the Civil Rights Monitor.

Janis Emplit, Advantica's senior vice president for information systems, presented the award in her area to Karen Bird, who oversees the restaurant systems area. Karen has been responsible for recruiting a diverse team of systems analysts to work on Y2K issues. She spoke movingly of the importance of difference to the effectiveness of working teams, quoting research from Nancy Kovach of the University of California, Los Angeles to support what all of us at Advantica know from personal experience.

Ron Hutchison, chief financial officer for Advantica, presented his area's award to Edward Holman, the company's director of corporate financial services. Edward, who's in charge of our databases, oversees a team of 110 employees who, in Ron's words, "are encouraged by Edward to participate to the fullest of their abilities, regardless of race, ethnicity, or gender. That's what's important here at Advantica."

Paul Wexler, who leads our work in the areas of procurement and distribution, gave the honor in his area to Maggie Petersen-Penn, who is director of supplier diversity. Maggie and her team, as you've read, are responsible for bringing $125 million worth of contracts with minority firms to Advantica—18% of our total contracts and five times the national average. "The supplier diversity program at Advantica is like a three-legged stool," Maggie said in her acceptance speech. "One leg represents the commitment and leadership of (her boss) Paul Wexler; another leg represents the hard work of the purchasing agents, the buyers, and the administrative staff. The other leg represents the minority procurement department. It is through this team that we're able to meet the goals and objectives Advantica has set for us."

Stephen Wood, executive vice president of human resources and corporate affairs, prefaced his presentation with an expression of personal pleasure: "As the company's chief people person," he said, "it's a genuine honor to work somewhere where people truly come first." He then presented his area's award to Aundrea Clark, whom he called "a master trainer, a trainer of trainers." It is Aundrea who took a lead role in the actual training of Advantica employees, as well as training those who train them. A 16-year veteran of the company, Aundrea's been a trainer for 4 years and concentrates now on special interventions—working in particularly difficult or resistant situations.

Aundrea was away in Memphis—training, of course— and couldn't receive his award personally. But he did tape a message of gratitude at being chosen as an Abrazo Achiever.

Ray then took the stage to present the award for her area to Linda Young, the national media manager for Denny's. It was Linda's work, in creating targeted media plans geared to specific segments of minority communities, that helped Denny's increase the number of African-American customers by 1 million within two years. Linda has been instrumental in creating similar media plans that focus on the Hispanic-American and Asian-Pacific American markets.

It was my privilege to close the awards ceremony, and I used that time to speak about my own fears and my own hopes. I wanted to remind the people who work for me about some of the despicable things that have happened in this nation recently—the murder of James Byrd in Texas, because he was black; the murder of Matthew Shepard, because he was gay; the rise of neo-Nazi behaviors on the part of seemingly ordinary young people.

I wanted them to know that these things frightened me. And I wanted to remind them all that during my first time on the stage in the Advantica auditorium, I said to the assembly that if there were only one rule here at Advantica, it would be that we had to be good to one another and be good to the customer.

"I hope we continue to live by that model," I told them. "Yes, we've made a lot of progress, but we've still got a long way to go. We've got to make a difference in this world. I don't fight this battle personally every day because it's right for the bottom line. I fight this battle because it's the morally right thing to do. I want to end up at a company that does things because they're morally right first—and that starts with how we treat one another."

I ended with a word to the Abrazo Achievers. "I can't tell you how proud I was to be sitting there, to be the leader of this company, and to be associated with such fine human beings."

I said those things to the award recipients, but I mean them about every one of our 60,000 employees. Yes, we've learned some hard lessons, and it's often been a struggle. But the days of embarrassment are over here at Advantica, as we take the lessons we learned and use them to reinvent our company. We're also sharing the lessons we have learned with corporate America. We get numerous calls from other companies asking how we have made the changes in our organization.

To help tell our story, we produced a documentary that chronicles our changes and what we've learned in the process. Last year, we also aired three television messages on the topic of racial diversity to spark thinking and honest discussion about the importance of racial diversity in this country (Figure 11.3).

Figure 11.3   Stills from Denny's diversity commercials that were part of a national campaign designed to foster discussions about race relations. The commercials were produced in partnership with Citigate Communications and The Chisholm–Mingo Group.

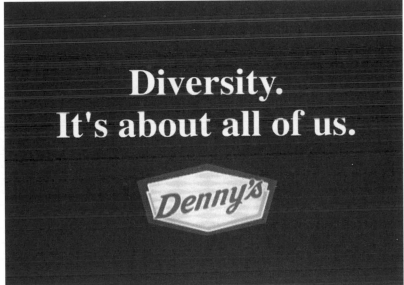

Figure 11.3   (*Continued*)

The commercial that received the most impact nationally was entitled, "I'm Black," and featured a young African-American male. The copy read:

> I want to let you in on a little secret. I'm black.
>
> There are some people who never notice another person's color.
>
> But most of us do. And that's OK. Don't feel guilty. Noticing a person's color doesn't make you a racist. Acting like it matters does.
>
> Some flowers are roses. Some are daisies.
>
> One's not automatically better than another. Just different.
>
> America is a garden. The more variety, the better.
>
> Diversity. It's about all of us.

We've done something that few companies in the United States can match; we've done it by caring about people, caring about excellence, and caring enough to do what's right. Who's coming to Denny's now? Just about everyone—and everyone is truly welcome at last.

Index

197